Abraham
LINCOLN
AND
Frederick
DOUGLASS

Abraham Lincoln and Frederick Douglass.

Abraham
LINCOLN
~ AND ~
Frederick
DOUGLASS

*The Story Behind
an American Friendship*

RUSSELL FREEDMAN

CLARION BOOKS
Houghton Mifflin Harcourt • Boston New York 2012

Clarion Books
215 Park Avenue South, New York, New York 10003

Clarion Books is an imprint of Houghton Mifflin Harcourt Publishing Company.

www.hmhbooks.com

The text was set in 13-point Berling.
Book design by Trish Parcell Watts

Library of Congress Cataloging-in-Publication Data
Freedman, Russell.
Abraham Lincoln and Frederick Douglass : the story behind an American friendship / by Russell
Freedman.
p. cm.
ISBN 978-0-547-38562-4
1. Lincoln, Abraham, 1809–1865—Juvenile literature. 2. Douglass, Frederick, 1818–1895—Juvenile
literature. 3. Presidents—United States—Biography—Juvenile literature. 4. African American
abolitionists—Biography—Juvenile literature. 5. Friendship—United States—Juvenile literature. I.
Title.
E457.905.F725 2012
973.7092'2—dc23
2011025953

Manufactured in China
LEO 10 9 8 7 6 5 4 3 2 1
4500343913

To Dick Mayer

for the gift of friendship

~ CONTENTS ~

The White House, around 1865.

~ ONE ~

Waiting for Mr. Lincoln

Heads turned when Frederick Douglass walked into the White House on the morning of August 10, 1863. It was still early, but the waiting area leading to Abraham Lincoln's office was crowded with politicians, officials, patronage seekers, and citizens of all kinds seeking an audience with the president.

Douglass was the only black man among them. The others seemed surprised to see him, and some were none too pleased.

Lincoln tried to meet with as many callers as he possibly could each day. He said he enjoyed his "public opinion baths" and found them a useful way to find out what people were thinking. When first elected, he had refused to limit his visiting hours. "They do not want much," he said of the throngs of citizens waiting to see him one day, "and they get very little. . . . I know how I would feel in their place."

But the crowds became unmanageable. People showed up before breakfast and were still waiting to see him late at night. At times, even U.S. senators had to wait a week or more to speak with the president. As his work piled up, Lincoln realized that he had to restrict his visiting hours. He saw callers from ten o'clock in the morning till one in the afternoon. Priority was given to cabinet members and congressmen; if any time remained, ordinary citizens were admitted.

It wasn't easy to see the president. Not everyone got in.

Douglass handed his calling card to a clerk and looked around for an empty chair. None was available, so he found a place to sit on the stairway leading to Lincoln's office. The stairs were filled with other men hoping for a moment with the nation's chief executive.

Douglass had no appointment. He had no idea how long he might have to wait, or even if he would be granted an interview. By meeting with the president, he hoped "to secure just and fair treatment" for the thousands of black troops who had enlisted in the Union army and were now fighting for the North in America's Civil War.

When the war began, federal law prohibited blacks from serving in the army. But as the fighting continued, with mounting casualties and no decisive victories, the North finally allowed African Americans to enlist. Black soldiers fought with distinction, but they were paid only half as much as white soldiers and were not being promoted for outstanding service. Worse, black prisoners of war were being executed or enslaved by their Southern captors.

Douglass had come to Washington to "lay the complaints of my people before President Lincoln." At forty-five, formally dressed for his visit, he was a commanding figure, taller than most men, with a powerful athlete's build, graying hair, penetrating brown eyes, and a carefully trimmed beard. A former slave, he had escaped to freedom and become a famous author, newspaper editor, and abolitionist. He had spent his career as a free man demanding that slavery be abolished in America and equal rights extended to whites and blacks alike.

Douglass and Lincoln had never met, but they had some things in common. They had both risen from poverty and obscurity to international prominence. Both were self-educated. Lincoln, born dirt poor, had less than a year of formal schooling. Douglass, born a slave, wasn't permitted to go to school. He taught himself to read and write in secret, hiding the few books he was able to get his hands on. And in fact the two men had read and studied some of the same books.

Even so, in the year 1863 it required plenty of "nerve," as Douglass put it, for a black man to walk unannounced into the White House and request an audience with the president.

Millions of blacks were still enslaved on farms and plantations in the Confederate South. In the North, African Americans were free but were denied many rights. Just a month earlier, rioters in New York, protesting the military draft, had beaten and lynched innocent blacks and burned the Colored Orphan Asylum to the ground.

"The distance between the black man and the white American citizen was immeasurable," Douglass later recalled. "I was an ex-slave, identified with a despised race, and yet I was to meet the most exalted person in this great republic. . . . I could not know what kind of reception would be accorded me. I might be told to go home and mind my business. . . . Or I might be refused an interview altogether."

He was determined to wait.

Slave children.

~ TWO ~

Born into Slavery

Born into slavery on a Maryland plantation, Frederick Douglass never knew exactly when his birthday was. "I have no accurate knowledge of my age," he wrote, "never having seen any authentic record containing it. By far the larger part of the slaves know as little of their ages as horses know of theirs, and it is the wish of most masters . . . to keep their slaves thus ignorant."

The question of his correct birth date and age plagued Douglass throughout his life. "The white children could tell their ages," he recalled. "I could not tell why I ought to be deprived of the same privilege. I was not allowed to make any inquiries of my master concerning it. He deemed all such inquiries on the part of a slave improper and impertinent, and evidence of a restless spirit."

According to a slave inventory by Frederick's owner—evidence that was

Feeding slave children, 1861. Illustration from Harper's Pictorial History of the Civil War.

unavailable to him—he was born in February 1818. His mother was a young slave named Harriet Bailey. "My father was a white man," he wrote. "He was admitted to be such by all I ever heard speak of my parentage." As with his age, the boy could never be quite certain who his father was. The name given to him by his mother was Frederick Augustus Washington Bailey.

As an infant he was placed in the care of his grandmother, who was too old for field labor. Frederick rarely saw his mother before she died, when he was about seven. She would visit him at night after finishing her day's work and lie down with him and hold him until he fell asleep. When he awoke, she was always gone. "She was a field hand," he wrote, "and a whipping is the penalty of not being in the field at sunrise."

Whippings of slaves became seared into the boy's memory. He remembered hiding terrified in a closet while his first owner, Aaron Anthony, was whipping Frederick's aunt Hester. "The louder she screamed, the harder he whipped, and where the blood ran fastest, there he whipped the longest. I was quite a child, but I well remember it. I never shall forget it whilst I remember anything. . . . I dared not venture out [of the closet] till long after the bloody transaction was over. I expected it would be my turn next."

When Aaron Anthony died, his son-in-law, Thomas Auld, became the boy's new owner.

Frederick must have been a very bright and appealing youngster. Before he was old enough to work in the fields, he was picked from among the other slave children and sent to Baltimore to live with the family of Hugh Auld, Thomas's brother. He would work as a houseboy for Auld's wife, Sophia, and help look after the couple's little son, Tommy.

Sophia Auld was a kindly person who had never before had a slave under her control. She decided to teach Frederick to read, but when her husband found out, he ordered her to stop the lessons at once. As Frederick stood by silently, Hugh Auld warned his wife that it was unlawful, as well as unsafe, to teach a slave to read. If the boy learned to read, "there would be no keeping him," said Hugh. "It would forever unfit him to be a slave. He would at once become unmanageable and of no value to his master. As to himself, it would do him no good, but a great deal of harm. It would make him discontented and unhappy."

Hugh's words came as a revelation to Frederick. "I now understood what had been to me a most perplexing difficulty—to wit, the white man's power to enslave the black man. . . . From that moment, I understood the pathway from slavery to freedom. . . . Though conscious of the difficulty of learning without a teacher, I set out with high hope, and a fixed purpose, at whatever cost of trouble, to learn how to read."

During the seven years that Frederick lived with the family of Hugh Auld, he taught himself to read and write. All that time he had to hide his efforts to learn. If he was caught with a newspaper or book, it was snatched away.

Advertising for slaves.

CASH!

All persons that have **SLAVES** to dispose of, will do well by giving me a call, as I will give the

HIGHEST PRICE FOR

Men, Women, & CHILDREN.

Any person that wishes to sell, will call at Hill's tavern, or at Shannon Hill for me, and any information they want will be promptly attended to.

Thomas Griggs.

Charlestown, May 7, 1835.

PRINTED AT THE FREE PRESS OFFICE, CHARLESTOWN.

He studied secretly. When he was left alone in the house, he studied the *Webster's Spelling Book* that Tommy had brought home from school. When he was sent out on errands, he made friends with the neighborhood white boys whom he met on the street. "As many of these as I could, I converted to teachers. With their kindly aid, obtained at different times and in different places, I finally succeeded in learning to read."

When the neighborhood boys talked about what they would be when they grew up, Frederick reminded them that he had no such choice. "You will be free as soon as you are twenty-one," he would say, "*but I am a slave for life!* Have not I as good a right to be free as you have?" Those words seemed to trouble his young white friends. They would express their sympathy and their hope that he would someday be free. "I do not remember ever to have met with a boy while I was in slavery, who defended the slave system," he wrote.

One of the neighborhood boys had a book called *The Columbian Orator*, a collection of speeches and dialogues about freedom, democracy, and courage compiled by Caleb Bingham, a Boston bookseller. This book, widely popular at the time, made a deep and lasting impression on young Frederick Bailey—"that gem of a book," he called it, "with its eloquent orations and spicy dialogues, denouncing oppression and slavery." With fifty cents he had somehow managed to save, he bought a secondhand copy of the book. When he was out on an errand, he would find a quiet spot where he could be alone. Then he would pull *The Columbian Orator* out of his pocket and read aloud, listening to the sound of his voice as he recited some of the great speeches of the past.

He read one selection, "Dialogue Between a Master and Slave," so many times, he could still quote from it decades later. The

THE

COLUMBIAN ORATOR:

CONTAINING A VARIETY OF

ORIGINAL AND SELECTED PIECES;

TOGETHER WITH

RULES,

CALCULATED

TO IMPROVE YOUTH AND OTHERS

IN THE ORNAMENTAL AND USEFUL

ART OF ELOQUENCE.

BY CALEB BINGHAM, A. M.

Author of the American Preceptor, Young Lady's Accidence, &c.

"CATO cultivated ELOQUENCE, as a necessary mean for defending
THE RIGHTS OF THE PEOPLE, and for enforcing good Counsels."
HOLLIN.

EIGHTEENTH EDITION.

New-York:

PUBLISHED BY E. DUYCKINCK, 102 PEARL-STREET.

J. C. Totten, printer.

1816.

Title page of The Columbian Orator, *first published in 1816.*

slave has been captured after running away for the third time. His master says that he has been kind and the slave should be grateful. The slave replies that kindness has nothing to do with it; he wants liberty. Each argument that the master puts forward in defense of slavery is dismissed by the slave with such power and conviction that in the end, the slave wins his freedom.

"The more I read, the more I was led to abhor and detest my enslavers. . . . That very discontent that Master Hugh had predicted would follow my learning to read had already come, to torment and sting my soul. . . . I would at times feel that learning to read had been a curse rather than a blessing. It had given me a view of my wretched condition, without the remedy. . . . From that time I resolved to run away."

Frederick was sent back to the plantation when he was fifteen and put to work for Thomas Auld, his owner. Thomas proved to be a harsh and unpredictable master, "cruel and hateful in all his ways." He found Frederick "unsuitable to his purpose. My city life, he said, had . . . almost ruined me. . . . Master Thomas at length said he would stand it no longer. I had lived with him nine months, during which time he had given me a number of severe whippings, all to no good purpose. He resolved to put me out, as he said, to be broken."

The boy was hired out as a field hand to Edward Covey, a professional "slave breaker," whose job was to beat troublesome young slaves into submission, much as horses are broken. Frederick was now, for the first time, a field hand. "I found myself even more awkward than a country boy appeared to be in a large city. I had been at my new home but one week before Mr. Covey gave me a very severe whipping."

Frederick lived with Covey for a year. With other slaves he labored in the fields from dawn to dusk. "We were worked in all weathers. It was never too hot or too cold; it could never rain, blow, hail, or snow too hard for us to work in the field." Frederick's lack of experience handling workhorses and farm tools infuriated Covey, who whipped the boy regularly.

On Sundays, when the slaves were not required to work, he would spend his leisure time "in a sort of beast-like stupor between sleep and wake, under some large tree. . . . I was sometimes prompted to take my life, and that of Covey, but was prevented by a combination of hope and fear."

He would walk to the shore of nearby Chesapeake Bay and watch "with saddened heart and tearful eye" the white sails moving toward the ocean beyond and wish that he were on one of those ships, heading for freedom: "O that I were free. I will run away. I will not stand it. . . . It cannot be that I shall live and die a slave. I will take to the water. The bay shall bear me into freedom."

After several months Frederick, now a strapping sixteen-year-old, found the courage to stand up to Covey and his bloody cowhide lash. One morning, when Covey was about to whip him again, "I resolved to fight, and . . . I seized Covey hard by the throat. . . . He held on to me, and I to him. My resistance was so entirely unexpected, that Covey seemed taken all aback. He trembled like a leaf."

They grappled and struggled and fell to the ground. "Covey at length let me go, puffing and blowing at a great rate, saying that if I had not resisted, he would not have whipped me at all."

From that time on, Covey never attempted to lay a finger on Frederick. He could have asked the sheriff to haul Frederick to the public whipping post and whip him for raising a hand against a white man. But he didn't. "The only explanation I can think of," Douglass wrote years later, "[is that] Mr. Covey enjoyed the most unbounded reputation for being a first-rate overseer and negro-breaker. . . . That reputation was at stake; and had he sent me—a boy about sixteen years old—to the public whipping post, his reputation would have been lost, so, to save his reputation, he suffered me to go unpunished."

When Frederick's year with Covey was up, the young slave was hired out to a neighboring planter named William Freeland. "My treatment, while in his employment, was heavenly compared with what I experienced at the hand of Mr. Edward Covey. . . . I went through [the year] without receiving a single blow." And yet Frederick found that the better his treatment, the more he felt the injustice of his servitude, and the greater his yearning for freedom. He resolved that before another year passed, he would attempt to escape.

He met secretly with five fellow slaves who agreed to join together in a flight to freedom. Their plan was to escape by water aboard a large canoe belonging to one of their masters. When they reached the head of Chesapeake Bay, about eighty miles away, they would cast the canoe adrift and continue traveling north by land, guided by the North Star.

But someone, they never knew who, betrayed them. On the morning of their planned escape, while they were working in the field, the horn was blown as usual, calling them to the house for breakfast. There they were seized, their hands lashed together, and dragged fifteen miles behind horses to the local jail, where "we all denied we ever intended to run away."

Frederick was released to the custody of Thomas Auld, who, "to my surprise and utter astonishment," decided to return the boy back to Baltimore, where he would live again with Hugh Auld and learn a trade. Even without evidence, the local slave owners believed that Frederick was the ringleader of a planned escape. "My master sent me away," he believed, "because there existed against me a very great prejudice in the community, and he feared I might be killed."

In Baltimore, Hugh Auld took Frederick to the shipyard where he worked as a foreman. The young slave was to be trained as a ship's caulker—a worker who packs the wooden seams of boats with pitch or other waterproof material. "In the course of one year I was able to command the highest wages paid to the most experienced caulkers." When there was no work to be had at

Baltimore as it appeared in 1837, when Frederick was working as a ship's caulker. From a painting by Moses Swett.

Auld's shipyard, he was allowed to seek employment at other yards. Even so, he was still a slave, so he had to turn all his earnings over to his master. "I earned it; yet upon returning [from work] Saturday night, I was compelled to deliver every cent of that money to Master Hugh."

Seeing that he could find employment on his own, Frederick went to Master Hugh with a proposal: He was earning a dollar and a half a day, sometimes more. If he were allowed to hire himself out but keep part of his wages, he could live on his own, pay his room and board, and buy his tools. In return for that liberty, he would pay Master Hugh three dollars at the end of every week. He would still be a slave under Maryland law but would be responsible for his own keep—a system widely practiced in Baltimore. "This arrangement was decidedly in my master's favor. It relieved him of all need of looking after me. . . . He received all the benefits of slaveholding without its evils. While I endured all the evils of a slave, and suffered all the care and anxiety of a freeman." Even so, "it was a step toward freedom to bear the responsibilities of a freeman."

Master Hugh agreed. He no longer needed Frederick to help look after his son, Tommy, now a teenager. He could profit from Frederick's work without having to feed and clothe him, and without losing possession of a valuable slave.

As for Frederick, the small taste of freedom he experienced as an independent worker "only increased my desire to be free, and set me to thinking of plans to gain my freedom."

Living independently, Frederick made friends among Baltimore's large community of free black people. He was invited to join a debating society made up of free black ship caulkers whom he knew from work. Frederick was the only slave belonging to the group. Reading a Baltimore newspaper, he learned that

Slaves on a South Carolina plantation, 1862.

a few reformers in the North, called "abolitionists," were "pleading for us" and "moving for our freedom." And he met people active in the Underground Railroad who helped move fugitive slaves along well-established escape routes, and who now helped Frederick Bailey work out his own escape plan.

He had fallen in love, meanwhile, with Anna Murray, a free black woman who worked as a maid, saved her money, taught him to play the violin, and encouraged his plans to escape. According to family tradition, Anna sold her featherbed to help pay for the train and ferry fares along Frederick's escape route. Once he made his way safely to the North, Anna was to join him and they would marry.

All free blacks had to carry documents while traveling to show that they were not slaves. Through his network of friends, Frederick obtained the papers of a free black seaman. He would impersonate a sailor. He was provided with the names of fellow blacks and antislavery whites who could be trusted to help him on his way north.

The risks ahead were great, and the price of failure terrible to contemplate: "If I failed in this attempt, my case would be a hopeless one—it would seal my fate as a slave forever. I could not hope to get off with anything less than the severest punishment, and being placed beyond the means of escape."

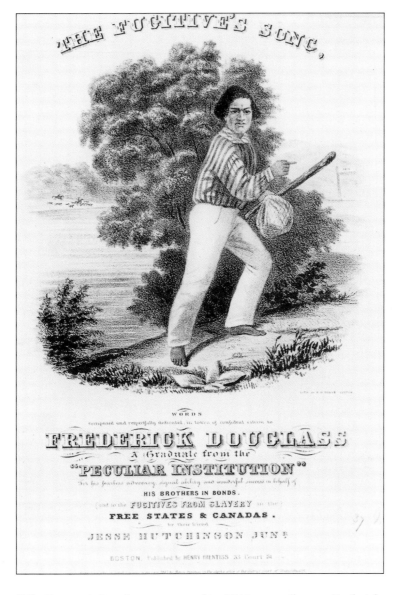

"The Fugitive's Song" was composed in 1845 as a tribute to Frederick Douglass and his "graduation" from the "peculiar institution," as slavery was sometimes called. Douglass is pictured on the sheet music cover as a runaway slave, fleeing barefoot from two mounted pursuers and a pack of dogs chasing him across the river.

— THREE —

Soul on Fire

On the morning of Monday, September 3, 1838, Frederick Bailey was delivered to the Baltimore train station in a horse-drawn cab driven by a friend. Dressed as a sailor, he wore a red shirt, a black kerchief tied loosely around his neck, and a sailor's flat-topped, broad-brimmed hat. In his pocket he carried the seaman's papers he had obtained, which described a man very different in appearance.

At the ticket window, he knew, his papers would be checked carefully. To avoid this scrutiny, he waited outside the station until the train to Wilmington, Delaware, was ready to pull out. When the conductor shouted, *"All aboard!"* Frederick's cab raced to the train and pulled up beside the coach set aside for black passengers. Bag in hand, Frederick jumped aboard just as the train got under way. He would buy his ticket on board.

As the train gained speed, he waited anxiously for the conductor to enter the coach to collect tickets and examine the papers of black passengers. "This was a critical moment. . . . My whole future depended on the decision of this conductor."

The conductor appeared. Frederick had to rely now "on the jostle of the train, and the natural haste of the conductor," who moved gruffly through the crowded black passenger car. When he reached Frederick, "to my surprise and relief, his whole manner changed." His expression brightened. Baltimore was a seafaring city, and sailors were popular.

"I suppose you have your free papers?"

"No, sir. I never carry my free papers to sea with me."

"But you have something to show that you are a free man, have you not?"

"Yes, sir. I have a paper with the American eagle on it, that will carry me round the world." Frederick pulled out his seaman's papers and handed them over. The large emblem of the American eagle at the top of the papers caught the conductor's eye, and he did not bother to read the description of the bearer below. Handing the papers back, he took Frederick's cash fare, punched a ticket, and moved on to the next passenger.

Frederick's journey was just beginning. While still in Maryland, subject to arrest as a fugitive at any moment, he had to board a ferry to cross the Susquehanna River, then continue north on another train. At Wilmington, still in slave country, he would change to a steamboat up the Delaware River to Philadelphia. Along the way he had two close calls.

Once he spotted a sea captain who patronized the shipyard where Frederick worked and would immediately recognize him as a slave. As they passed each other, the captain seemed preoccupied. He did not notice Frederick.

"But this was not [my] only hairbreadth escape. A German

blacksmith, whom I knew well, was on the train [to Wilmington] with me, and looked at me very intently, as if he thought he had seen me somewhere before in his travels. I really believed he knew me, but had no heart to betray me. At any rate he saw me escaping, and held his peace."

Arriving in Philadelphia, a free city, Frederick went immediately onto another ferry, then boarded a night train, and then a final ferry that carried him to New York City. When he stepped off the boat early in the morning of September 4, he recalled, "it was a moment of the highest excitement I ever experienced. . . . I felt like one who had escaped from a den of hungry lions."

He was twenty years old. In less than twenty-four hours and not quite two hundred miles, he had transformed himself from a slave to a free man.

Yet the "hurrying throng" and the "dazzling wonders of Broadway" harbored risks and dangers that could bring this glorious moment to an abrupt and ugly end. New York was a profitable hunting ground for professional slave catchers, legalized kidnappers constantly on the lookout for runaways, ready to capture fugitive slaves and return them to their owners in exchange for ample rewards. "I was yet liable to be taken back and subjected to all the tortures of slavery," Frederick remembered. "I was afraid to talk to anyone for fear of talking to the wrong one."

He found his way to the safe haven of David Ruggles's house, a few blocks from the ferry pier. Ruggles was a free black journalist who headed the New York branch of the Underground Railroad, which protected fugitive slaves and helped them make their way farther north. He advised Frederick to pick a new name to help avoid detection. He chose "Frederick Johnson."

Then he wrote to Anna to join him in New York. On September 15, eleven days after Frederick's escape, they were married in David Ruggles's parlor by the Reverend James W. C. Pennington, another runaway slave from Maryland and a newly ordained Presbyterian minister. Anna wore a "new plum-colored silk dress." Frederick put on the wrinkled suit he had carried in his seaman's bag especially for the wedding. With their marriage certificate in hand and five dollars from David Ruggles to help pay their train and ferry fares, "I shouldered one part of our baggage and Anna took up the other." They set off for New Bedford, Massachusetts, where, Ruggles had promised, Frederick could find work at his ship caulker's trade.

New Bedford, a prospering seaport and the nation's whaling capital, had a sizable community of free blacks. Frederick and Anna moved into a small apartment near the wharves. A neighbor, Nathan Johnson, suggested that Frederick again change his name, since there were already too many Johnsons in town. Frederick finally settled on "Douglas," after James Douglas, a character in Sir Walter Scott's poem *Lady of the Lake*. Frederick was familiar with Douglass Street in Baltimore, so when he adopted the new name he spelled it with an extra *s*. Frederick Douglass now, he left Frederick Bailey behind for good.

When he applied for work at a local shipyard, he found that New Bedford, despite its diverse population, had its share of racism. The white workers threatened to quit if Frederick was hired as a skilled caulker. They agreed to let him work as a day laborer instead, at half their pay. For the next three years he labored at any kind of job he could find—sawing wood, shoveling coal, sweeping chimneys, rolling oil casks, working at a brass foundry. The work was hard and often dirty, but "I was now my own master. . . . It was the first work, the reward of which was to be entirely my own. There was no master Hugh, standing ready, the moment I earned the money, to rob me of it," he wrote.

At the wharf in Newport, Rhode Island, Frederick and his bride, Anna, changed from a steamboat to a stagecoach headed for New Bedford, Massachusetts. Illustration from Life and Times of Frederick Douglass, *published in 1881.*

Frederick Douglass's New Bedford waterfront.

Frederick and Anna moved to a small house and started a family, raising two daughters and three sons. They joined New Bedford's Zion Chapel, a congregation of black Methodists. Frederick subscribed to the *Liberator,* a weekly paper published in Boston by the Massachusetts Anti-Slavery Society.

The *Liberator* called for an immediate end to slavery and demanded equal rights for all people. The paper was banned throughout the South. In Georgia the legislature had offered a $5,000 reward for the arrest of its editor, the abolitionist William Lloyd Garrison. Frederick "mastered" every issue, as he put it. "The paper became my meat and my drink. My soul was set all on fire."

Inspired by the *Liberator,* he began to attend abolitionist meetings. "I could do but little; but what I could, I did with a joyful heart, and never felt happier than when in an anti-slavery meeting. I seldom had much to say at the meetings, because what I wanted to say was said so much better by others."

In 1841, three years after arriving in New Bedford, Frederick traveled to Nantucket to attend a two-day convention of the Massachusetts Anti-Slavery Society. Urged to "say a few words," he summoned his courage and rose to address the biggest audience he had ever faced—more than five hundred abolitionists, most of them white. "The truth was, I felt myself a slave, and the idea of speaking to white people, weighed me down."

"It was with the utmost difficulty that I could stand erect," Frederick recalled. Hesitating and stammering, "I trembled in every limb. I am not sure that my embarrassment was not the most effective part of my speech, if speech it could be called. At any rate, this is about the only part of my performance that I distinctly remember."

Speaking haltingly at first, he overcame his nervousness, and then the words poured forth. His audience would never forget that evening. They sat in rapt attention as they watched this earnest young black man and heard his passionate words. It was clear to everyone that a powerful new voice had been raised, and before the convention adjourned, Frederick was invited to become a paid speaker of the Massachusetts Anti-Slavery Society, to go out on the lecture circuit and tell the world about his life as a slave.

Twenty-three-year-old Frederick Douglass had found his calling. After he returned home to New Bedford, he set out on tour. During the next few years, he traveled constantly by train and stagecoach, lecturing at antislavery meetings in cities and

Frederick Douglass around 1847. This is believed to be the earliest photograph taken of him.

towns throughout the Eastern and Midwestern United States.

Making more than a hundred appearances a year, Douglass became a magnetic speaker, adding humor, sarcasm, and mimicry to his graphic accounts of the horrors of human bondage. He dressed formally, and his chiseled features and impassioned eloquence cast a spell on audiences "that laughed and wept by turns, completely carried away by the wondrous gifts of his pathos and humor."

Usually, Frederick traveled with John Collins, a white lecturer. While slavery was outlawed in the North, racial discrimination was common. Trains in Massachusetts were segregated, with black passengers assigned to separate cars, sometimes the freight car. Once, when Douglass and Collins were traveling together, the conductor ordered Douglass to move to the "colored car." Douglass refused. The conductor rounded up several toughs who wrestled Douglass from his seat and threw him off the train at the next stop.

Moving from town to town, Douglass and Collins spoke in churches, schools, and barns, or out-of-doors in parks and on town greens when every door "stood locked and bolted against us." When Frederick arrived in a town by himself, he often had trouble finding a place to speak. In Grafton, Massachusetts, he borrowed a dinner bell from a hotel and walked through town ringing the bell and crying out, "*Notice!* Frederick Douglass, recently a slave, will lecture on American slavery on Grafton Common this evening at 7 o'clock." A large crowd turned out to hear him, and the next day a local church opened its doors to him.

Antislavery speakers were often heckled. People threw rotten eggs at them, and at times their message incited violence. In Pendleton, Indiana, Douglass and two white lecturers were attacked by an angry mob. Douglass was hit with a club and his

right hand broken before the attackers got on their horses and rode off. Despite his injuries, he lectured the next day. His hand was not properly set and bothered him for the rest of his life.

As he toured the country, people questioned whether he really, in truth, had been a slave. He didn't seem to look, act, or speak like a slave. "Many persons in the audience . . . could not believe that he was actually a slave," wrote a Philadelphia reporter. "How

In this rare daguerreotype, Douglass is seen seated (center right) on the speakers' platform at an antislavery gathering in Cazenovia, New York, August 1850. Standing just behind him is the prominent abolitionist Gerrit Smith, who would later run for president.

Fighting off the mob. Illustration from Life and Times of Frederick Douglass, *1881.*

a man, only six years out of bondage, and who had never gone to school a day in his life, could speak with such eloquence—with such precision of language and power of thought—they were utterly at a loss to devise."

To answer such doubts, Douglass wrote the book that would make him famous. In 1845, when he was twenty-seven, he published his autobiography *Narrative of the Life of Frederick Douglass, an American Slave: Written by Himself*—the first of three autobiographies he would write in his lifetime. So eloquent was the book, so graphic its accounts of slavery, skeptics argued that it could not possibly have been written by a black man, certainly not by a runaway slave. Published in Europe as well as the United States, the book became an international bestseller. An American reviewer called it "the most thrilling work which the American press ever issued—*and the most important!*"

In his lectures, Douglass had been careful not to reveal details about where he came from and who had owned him. He was still a fugitive, subject to capture and return to his owner. But his book named dates, places, and people; it was clear that the author was the runaway slave named Frederick Bailey.

His friends worried that if Thomas or Hugh Auld saw the book, they would attempt to hunt Frederick down and get their "property" back. Under the law, Massachusetts could do nothing to protect him. Hugh did, in fact, manage to read the *Narrative*, even though it was banned everywhere in the South. He vowed to "spare no pains or expense in order to regain possession of him [Frederick]" and "place him in the cotton fields of the South."

Frederick's friends urged him to sail to Great Britain, as other fugitive slaves had done. There he would be safe from arrest and could support himself by lecturing.

Three months after his *Narrative* was published, Douglass fled to the British Isles, which had abolished slavery. Greeted as a celebrity, he spent almost two years lecturing to enthusiastic audiences in England, Scotland, and Ireland, and forming a number of close friendships. Some of his English friends contacted Thomas Auld, Douglass's legal owner, and paid him just over $700 (about $17,000 in today's currency) in exchange for Frederick's freedom. When Douglass returned to Massachusetts in 1847, he was legally a free man.

An antislavery meeting in London. From an 1841 engraving by Henry Melville. Douglass toured the British Isles for two years, lecturing to large, enthusiastic crowds.

Famous as a writer and lecturer, Douglass now wanted to broadcast his ideas as widely as possible. He moved his family to Rochester, New York, a flourishing young city and a stronghold of antislavery activities. He bought a printing press, started his own abolitionist newspaper, and launched a new career as a journalist. His paper, the first of several he would publish over the years, was called the *North Star*, a reference to the beck-

oning star that guided runaway slaves as they made their way north.

The *North Star* called for universal emancipation of slaves and championed other causes, such as women's rights and the desegregation of schools. The paper's motto became "All rights for all."

"Justice must be done," Frederick Douglass declared, "the truth must be told. . . . I will not be silent."

A reconstruction of the log cabin on Knob Creek, Kentucky,
where Lincoln lived as a child.

— FOUR —

Nothing but Plenty of Friends

By 1848, Frederick Douglass was the most famous black man in America. Abraham Lincoln was an obscure congressman from Illinois, almost unknown beyond his home state.

Lincoln had little firsthand knowledge of slavery. As a young man, on two brief riverboat trips to New Orleans, he had glimpsed that city's teeming slave markets. And when he arrived in Washington as a first-term congressman, he was offended and embarrassed by the flourishing slave trade in the heart of the nation's capital. But he had spent most of his life in Indiana and Illinois, free states with small black populations, and as a newly elected member of the U.S. House of Representatives, he took almost no part in the heated debates over slavery and the growing antislavery movement in Congress.

Like Frederick Douglass, whom he had yet to meet, Lincoln took pride in being a "self-made man"—an expression coined in the 1830s that quickly caught on. Born in a humble log cabin near Hodgenville, Kentucky, on February 12, 1809, he had grown up on a succession of hardscrabble frontier homesteads.

Abraham was seven, and hadn't yet learned to read, when his father, Thomas, pulled up stakes and moved his little family from the backwoods of Kentucky to the untracked wilderness of Indiana. At times during their journey on horseback, Thomas had to hack out a path through thick underbrush so that Abraham, his older sister, Sarah, and their mother, Nancy, could follow.

Thomas had claimed a homestead on Little Pigeon Creek in southern Indiana. He built a temporary shelter of logs and boughs, enclosed on three sides, with the open side protected only by a roaring fire to fend off the winter winds and wild animals. Wolves and bears prowled the forests, and as Abraham remembered, "The panther's scream, filled night with fear."

Already big for his age, Abraham helped his father build a proper log cabin. When spring came, they planted their first crop of corn. Soon some of Nancy's kinfolk came to settle at Little Pigeon Creek, along with their adopted son, eighteen-year-old Dennis Hanks. Dennis took a liking to Abraham and became the boy's companion, like an older brother.

Then a mysterious illness called the milk sickness swept through the Little Pigeon Creek community, carrying off several settlers. When Dennis Hanks's family died, he moved in with the Lincolns. Nancy Hanks Lincoln also came down with the disease and suffered for a week. Abraham was nine when his mother passed away. Thomas sawed rough boards to make a coffin, Abraham whittled the pegs that held the wooden planks together, and the dead woman lay in the same one-room cabin where the family ate and slept. The next morning Nancy was buried on a windy hill beneath trees ablaze with the reds and golds of autumn.

A year later, Thomas went back to Kentucky and returned with a new wife, a widow named Sarah Bush Johnston, and her three children, who ranged in age from eight to thirteen. Now eight people were living in the smoky one-room Lincoln log cabin.

A poor white boy, Abe, as everyone called him, was often rented out by his father to work for neighboring settlers. He felled trees, split fence rails, plowed fields. At the end of the week he turned every cent he had earned over to his father, according to law and custom.

When he could be spared from his chores, he went to one of the log-cabin schools in the neighborhood. For Abe and his sister, Sarah, school was a sometime thing, a few weeks one winter, a month, maybe, the next. One school was four miles away. Abe would walk through groves of scrub trees and across creek bottoms carrying his homemade copybook, wearing his coonskin cap and buckskin trousers that were always too short for his growing legs. Lincoln figured that all his schooling "did not amount to one year."

Mostly, he educated himself. He discovered that he loved to read. He could lose himself in a book and imagine other worlds, and once he got the hang of it, he read all the books he could lay his hands on. "It didn't seem natural, nohow, to see a feller read like that," Dennis Hanks recalled.

Because books were scarce on the frontier, Abe might read a book he liked more than once. He read *Aesop's Fables* so many times, he could write it out from memory.

At sixteen Lincoln stood six feet two inches tall—a gangly youth with unruly black hair, big bony hands, and amazingly long legs. At eighteen he reached his full height of six feet four,

Abe discovered that he loved to read. From an 1868 painting by Eastman Johnson titled An Evening in the Log Hut.

unusually tall for that time. Years of swinging an ax had given him arm muscles like steel cables. He could take a heavy ax by the handle and hold it straight out at arm's length, nice and easy and steady, without even a quiver. "He can sink an ax deeper into wood than any man I ever saw," a neighbor said.

He was nineteen before he had a chance to break away from backwoods Indiana and see something of the world. Abe and a neighbor boy were hired to take a flatboat loaded with farm produce down the Ohio and Mississippi Rivers all the way to New Orleans, a three-month, 1,200-mile journey. New Orleans was

the first real city the two country boys had ever seen, and there
Lincoln had his first encounter with large numbers of slaves. The
city was the biggest slave-trading center in North America. Lincoln never forgot the sight of black men, women, and children
being driven along the streets, their chains clanking on the cobblestones, and being auctioned off like cattle. "The horrid pictures are in my mind yet," he said twenty years later.

In 1830, Thomas Lincoln decided to pull up stakes again and
move on to fertile new land in Illinois. Abe went along, driving
two yoke of oxen that pulled a wagon crammed with household
goods across the Wabash River and through the forests to a tract
of windswept prairie along the banks of the Sangamon River. He
helped his father build another log cabin, clear fifteen acres, and
split the rails to fence them in.

Lincoln was twenty-one now, of legal age and free to strike
out on his own. It was time to leave his father's household for
good. Offered a chance to take another flatboat loaded with farm
goods downriver to New Orleans, he readily accepted. When he
returned to Illinois, he paid a quick visit to his father and stepmother, gathered his belongings, and headed for the flourishing
village of New Salem, Illinois, where he had been promised a job
as a clerk in a general store.

Lincoln showed up in New Salem in the summer of 1831, "a
friendless, uneducated, penniless boy," as he later described himself, who had finally "separated from his father."

New Salem, with a population of a hundred or more, was the
largest community in which Lincoln had ever lived. He fit in easily. Like his father, he enjoyed cracking jokes and spinning yarns.
Folks liked his endless collection of stories, which he would spin
out at great length, gesturing with his hands and mimicking the
voices of his characters.

*This photograph is traditionally accepted
as a portrait of Lincoln's father, Thomas.*

Young Lincoln worked as a raftsman on the Ohio River, as pictured in this undated German engraving. In 1828 Abe and a friend floated a flatboat loaded with farm produce 1,200 miles down the Ohio and Mississippi Rivers to New Orleans.

He was welcomed into the New Salem debating club, and while he was awkward and self-conscious at first, he quickly grew more confident. In one debate, "he pursued the question with reason and argument so pithy and forcible that all were amazed," a fellow debater remembered.

Lincoln had discovered *The Columbian Orator*—the same popular book of speeches and dialogues that twelve-year-old Frederick Bailey was secretly reading in Baltimore at the same time. Like Frederick, Abraham found that the book was a wonderful self-help manual for speaking and debating. *The Columbian Orator* helped teach both Frederick in Maryland and Abraham in Illinois how to achieve success in the art of public speaking. Pronunciation was crucial, wrote Caleb Bingham, the book's author. "The more natural the pronunciation is, the more moving it will be, since the perfection of art consists in its nearest resemblance to nature."

During the six years Lincoln lived in New Salem, he was a young man in search of a career. He knew that he did not want to spend his life as a backwoods farmer, like his father. But he wasn't sure what he wanted to do. He tried his luck as a merchant, opening a general store with a partner, but after a few months the store "winked out," as Lincoln put it, leaving him with a debt that took fifteen years to pay off.

To tide himself over, he split fence rails, slaughtered hogs, helped out at the local gristmill. When an Indian war broke out in Illinois in 1832, he volunteered for the local militia, drilled and marched for three months, but never did sight any hostile Indians.

"Lincoln had nothing, only plenty of friends," one of those friends remembered. With a little help from his friends, he was appointed village postmaster, a part-time job that didn't pay enough to live on but gave him plenty of time to read all the newspapers that came in. If customers failed to pick up their mail at the post office, Lincoln would sometimes walk miles to deliver the mail in person.

When he was offered the chance to become an assistant to the local surveyor, he bought a compass and a couple of textbooks and "went at it," teaching himself enough surveying to start work—laying out roads and town sites and marking off property boundaries.

His friends urged him to become a candidate for the state legislature. Why not? Everyone in New Salem knew him, and he was well liked. The first time he ran, he came in eighth in a field of thirteen candidates. But he tried again two years later, and in 1834, at the age of twenty-five, Lincoln was elected after conducting a hand-shaking campaign all over the county where his surveying work had taken him.

He borrowed enough money to buy the first suit he had ever

Slave auction in the American South. An 1862 illustration from a French magazine.

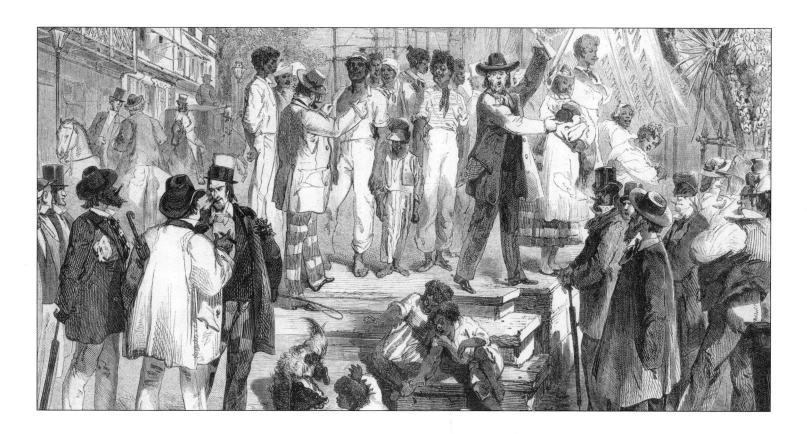

Lincoln reading law books. From a painting by an unidentified artist, c. 1934.

owned and set out in a stagecoach for the Illinois state capital at Vandalia, where he became the second-youngest member of the legislature.

State legislators were paid very little, and only when the legislature was in session, so Lincoln still had to make a living. A fellow legislator, a young attorney named John Todd Stuart, advised him to take up the study of law—an ideal profession for a young man with political ambitions. The law would give him a chance to rise in the world, to avoid a life of hard physical labor. He had served as a juror in the Sangamon County Circuit Court, been called twice as a witness, and seen for himself the give-and-take of legal argument and the informal procedures of the local court.

Yet Lincoln hesitated, because he had so little formal education. Not a problem, Stuart told him. Many leading lawyers at the time had never been to law school; instead, they "read law" in the office of a practicing attorney until they knew enough to pass their exams.

So just as he had taught himself surveying, Lincoln now studied law on his own. Borrowing law books from Stuart, he "went at it in good earnest," while serving in the state legislature and working as a surveyor when the legislature wasn't in session. "He read so much—was so studious—too[k] so little physical exercise—was so laborious in his studies," a friend observed, "that he became emaciated and his best friends were afraid that he would craze himself."

Lincoln read law books and memorized legal codes and precedents for nearly three years before passing his exams. He was admitted to practice on March 1, 1837. Meanwhile, he was reelected to a second term in the Illinois legislature, which was preparing to move from Vandalia to the new state capital at Springfield.

As a young state legislator Lincoln went on record for the first time concerning slavery, which in the Southern states was protected by law. Illinois was a free state—slavery was outlawed—but like most Northern states, it had laws intended to keep free blacks in their place. Blacks in Illinois could not vote, hold political office, sit on juries, or attend public schools, even though they had to pay taxes like everyone else. And while many whites in Illinois said they opposed slavery, they were willing to leave slavery alone in those states where it already existed. Most whites at the time regarded abolitionists as dangerous radicals.

In 1837 the Illinois legislature overwhelmingly passed a resolution declaring that "the right of property in slaves, is sacred to the slave-holding States [and guaranteed] by the Federal Constitution." Only two legislators—Lincoln and Dan Stone, a former Vermonter—opposed the resolution and voted no. They voiced their belief "that the institution of slavery is founded on both injustice and bad policy."

At the same time, however, Lincoln and Stone opposed the outright abolition of slavery. They agreed with their fellow legislators that the spread "of abolitionist doctrines tends rather to increase than to abate [slavery's] evils."

Lincoln was aware that, in 1837, a strong stand to abolish slavery could put an end to his career as a rising young Illinois politician.

As a member of the Illinois State Assembly, Lincoln was paid only when the legislature was in session. This check for ten dollars was for the session of 1834–35.

These daguerreotypes, the earliest known photographs of Abraham Lincoln and Mary Todd, were taken in 1846, when Lincoln had just been elected to Congress.

～ FIVE ～

A House Divided

On April 15, 1837, Lincoln rode into the new Illinois state capital at Springfield on a borrowed horse with seven dollars in his pocket. He was twenty-eight years old, a newly licensed attorney, a member of the state legislature, and ambitious to get ahead.

Working as a junior partner with John Todd Stuart, he helped build one of the busiest law practices in Springfield. Meanwhile he twice more won reelection to the legislature, serving four terms altogether.

In 1842, after a three-year courtship, Lincoln married Mary Ann Todd, a cousin of his law partner. Mary was ten years younger than Lincoln, fourteen inches shorter, witty, vivacious, and fashionably plump. She was attracted, she said, by his ambition, by his awkward shyness around eligible young women, and by "the most congenial mind" she had ever met. A few days after the wedding Lincoln wrote to a friend: "Nothing new here, except my marrying, which to me, is a matter of profound wonder."

Prospering as an attorney, Lincoln opened his own law office and took on talkative young William Herndon as his partner. Herndon was nine years Lincoln's junior and had just been licensed to practice. He addressed his partner as "Mr. Lincoln," while Lincoln called him "Billy." Even so, the two men shared equally in both the legal work they performed and the fees they collected.

When Lincoln arrived at the office in the morning, "the first thing he did was to pick up a newspaper, spread himself out on an old sofa, one leg on a chair, and read aloud, much to my discomfort," Herndon recalled. Lincoln once explained to him, "When I read aloud two senses catch the idea: first, I *see* what I read; second, I *hear* it, and therefore I can remember it better."

Impressed by Lincoln's slow, deliberate, methodical manner of thinking about a question, Herndon was convinced that his partner thought more than any man in America. "He can sit and think without food or rest longer than any man I ever met," Herndon said. According to his law partner, Lincoln was "pitiless and persistent in pursuit of truth" because he was little influenced by others and preferred to work out his own conclusions.

In 1846 Lincoln set his sights on a seat in Congress. He won his party's nomination easily and was elected to the U.S. House of Representatives by the biggest majority ever recorded in that congressional district. The important issues that year were the war being fought between the United States and Mexico and the spread of slavery beyond the Southern states. By the time Lincoln took his seat in Congress, American troops had marched into Mexico City. The Mexican government was about to sign a peace treaty surrendering huge chunks of its territory, including the present states of California, Nevada, and Utah, most of Arizona and New Mexico, and parts of Wyoming and Colorado.

Lincoln was an outspoken critic of the Mexican War, denouncing that conflict as a plot to seize vast new territories for the expansion of slavery. He supported a bill to prohibit slavery in all the territories taken from Mexico. And he proposed a bill of his own to gradually end slavery in the nation's capital, which met with so much opposition that he finally withdrew it. Aside from that, he took almost no part in the heated debates over slavery and the growing antislavery movement in Congress.

Slaves wearing handcuffs and leg shackles walk past the U.S. Capitol in this illustration from A Popular History of the United States, *published in 1876–81.*

He had said many times that he was "naturally antislavery. . . . I cannot remember a time when I did not so think and feel." But he believed that Congress had no power under the U.S. Constitution to interfere with slavery in those states where it already existed. And he feared that any efforts to force abolition on the South would only lead to violence. An antislavery congressman

Street fighting in the Mexican War. From an illustration by Henry Alexander Ogden (1856–1936).

remarked that Lincoln "had rather timid ideas about how to deal with the South."

Lincoln's opposition to the Mexican War wasn't popular among Illinois voters, and when his congressional term was over, he did not run again and returned to the full-time practice of law. For the next five years he stayed out of politics. But while he concentrated on his law practice, the future of slavery in America was becoming a divisive issue, splitting the nation and inciting violent conflict in the vast territories that were opening in the West.

Powerful interests in both the South and the North were determined to control the fate of the western territories. The South was seeking new lands for the large-scale cultivation of cotton and other crops by slave labor. The North demanded that the western territories be reserved for the free labor of independent farmers and workers, who should not have to compete with unpaid slave labor. As each territory reached statehood, the question became, would it enter the Union as a free state or a slave state?

The Missouri Compromise, passed by Congress in 1820, had managed to keep the peace by permitting slavery in some western territories and banning it in others. But by the 1840s that uneasy compromise was beginning to unravel. Growing numbers of Northerners regarded slavery as a moral evil that should not be allowed to spread. Southerners claimed a "sacred" right to own Negroes as slaves. They were determined to protect their way of life and spread slavery westward as new lands opened for settlement. Rather than an evil, one Southern senator declared, slavery was "a great moral, social, and political blessing—a blessing to the slave, and a blessing to the master."

The Kansas-Nebraska Act, passed by a bitterly divided

Congress in 1854, brought matters to a head. Under the Missouri Compromise, slavery had been barred from the territories of Kansas and Nebraska. Under this new act, the future of slavery in those territories would be determined not by Congress, but by the people who settled there. Under the doctrine of "popular sovereignty," the settlers would decide for themselves whether to enter the Union as free states or slave states.

Lincoln, along with many others, had expected that if slavery were confined to the South, it would eventually die out. Perhaps it could be legislated out of existence, with some sort of compen-

This 1856 political cartoon depicts the violence directed against antislavery settlers in Kansas, known as "freesoilers," following passage of the Kansas-Nebraska Act.

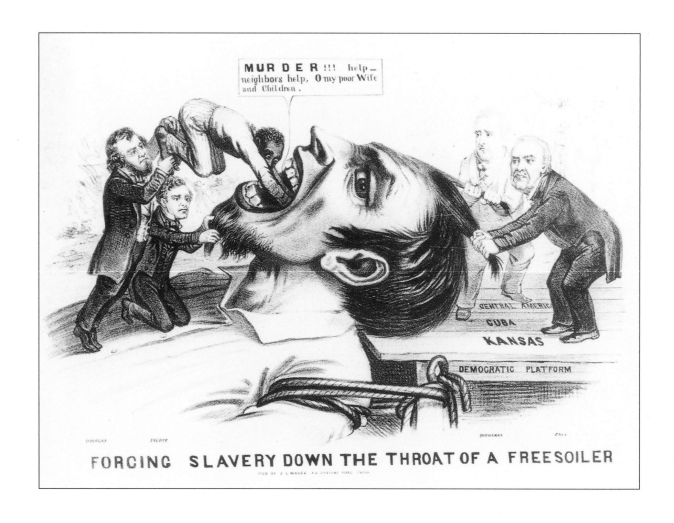

FORCING SLAVERY DOWN THE THROAT OF A FREESOILER

sation given to the slave owners in exchange for their property. As long as Congress kept slavery from spreading, Lincoln believed, it would gradually die a "natural death."

The Missouri Compromise had held slavery in check. But now that compromise had been overturned, causing a storm of protest in the North. The Kansas-Nebraska Act had opened the gates for slavery to expand and grow and establish itself permanently. Now it would never die the "natural death" Lincoln had expected.

"The Kansas-Nebraska Act took us by surprise—astounded us," Lincoln said. "We were thunderstruck and stunned." He had been losing interest in politics, but now he was aroused as he "had never been aroused before." For the first time in five years, he neglected his law practice to travel across Illinois, campaigning for antislavery candidates.

Plunging back into the political arena, Lincoln expressed a new tone of moral outrage as he attacked "the monstrous injustice of slavery." "There can be no moral right in connection with one man's making a slave of another," he declared.

While he opposed the spread of slavery, he confessed that he did not know what to do about those Southern states where slavery was already established, where it was protected by state and national laws. "If all earthly power were given me," he admitted, "I should not know what to do, as to the existing institution."

The controversy over slavery was escalating into violence. Kansas had become a battleground of burnings, lynchings, and rigged elections as proslavery Southerners and antislavery Northerners fought for control of the territory. And the violence spilled over onto the floor of the U.S. Senate. Representative Preston Brooks of South Carolina, enraged by Massachusetts Senator Charles Sumner's antislavery speech "The Crime Against Kansas," attacked Sumner with his gold-headed cane, beat him thirty times or more over the head, and almost killed him.

In 1857 the U.S. Supreme Court handed down a decision that shocked and dismayed the opponents of slavery. The court ruled that Congress had no power to prohibit slavery in *any* of the territories, because that would violate the property rights guaranteed by the Constitution.

The ruling concerned the fate of Dred Scott, a Missouri slave who sued for his freedom on the grounds that his owner had taken him onto free soil in the North. The court declared that as a black man, Scott was not a citizen of the United States and was not entitled to the rights spelled out by the Declaration of Independence. Slaves were private property, the court said, and Congress could not pass laws depriving white citizens of their property rights.

Antislavery forces throughout the North denounced the Dred Scott decision. Speaking in Springfield, Lincoln declared that the opinion did "obvious violence to the plain unmistakable language of the Declaration" of Independence, distorting that language "till, if its framers could rise from their graves, they could not at all recognize it." The authors of the Declaration never intended "to say all were equal in color, size, intellect, moral development or social capacity," Lincoln continued, but they "did consider all men created equal—equal in certain inalienable rights, among which are life, liberty, and the pursuit of happiness."

While Lincoln attacked the opinion, he urged respect for the courts. "We think the Dred Scott decision is erroneous," he said. "We know that court that made it, has often overruled its own decisions, and we should do what we can to have it overrule this."

Lincoln wanted to be in office again so he could influence

Dred Scott, a slave who sued for his freedom, is shown with his wife and daughters in this front-page newspaper story.

public policy. In 1858 he made a bid for the U.S. Senate as the candidate of the new Republican Party, founded four years earlier to combat the expansion of slavery. His opponent was Illinois Senator Stephen Douglas, a prominent leader of the Democratic Party and sponsor of the Kansas-Nebraska Act, which had opened the floodgates to the expansion of slavery.

Lincoln launched his campaign with a dynamic speech before twelve hundred sweltering, shirtsleeved, cheering delegates at the Republican convention in Springfield on the muggy evening of June 16, 1858. The critical issue for the country, Lincoln warned, was the spread of slavery across the nation and into the future. Unless the opponents of slavery stopped its westward expansion and put slavery back on the "course of ultimate extinction," slavery would spread its grip across the entire nation.

"A house divided against itself cannot stand," Lincoln declared.

"I believe this government cannot endure, permanently half *slave* and half *free*.

"I do not expect the Union to be *dissolved*—I do not expect the house to *fall*—but I *do* expect it will cease to be divided.

"It will become *all* one thing, or *all* the other.

"Either the *opponents* of slavery will . . . place it where the public mind shall rest in the belief that it is in the course of ultimate extinction, or its *advocates* will push it forward, till it shall become alike lawful in *all* the States, *old* as well as *new—North* as well as *South*."

With his "House Divided" speech, Lincoln emerged as a leading antislavery spokesman. In Rochester, New York, Frederick Douglass took note of the speech. "Well and wisely said," Douglass wrote. "Liberty or Slavery must become the law of the land."

And in fact, Douglass had been preaching the same message for several years, sometimes in almost the same words. "Liberty

and slavery cannot dwell together forever in the same country," Douglass declared. "One or the other of these must go to the wall. The South must either give up slavery, or the North must give up liberty. . . . They are as opposite as light and darkness—as Heaven and Hell."

Lincoln in 1858, when he delivered his "House Divided" speech.

Senator Stephen A. Douglas.

— SIX —

Debating the Future of Slavery in America

Lincoln's "House Divided" speech set the stage for his historic confrontation with Illinois senator Stephen Douglas during the election campaign of 1858. Lincoln was after Douglas's Senate seat. When the candidates met in a series of public debates, their opposing views were unmistakable.

"I do not regard the Negro as my equal," Douglas declared. "This government of ours is founded on the white basis. It was made by the white man, for the benefit of the white man, to be administered by white men."

"Let us discard all this quibbling about this man and the other man— this race and that race and the other race being inferior," Lincoln replied. "Let us discard all these things, and unite as one people throughout this land, until we shall once more stand up declaring that all men are created equal."

Douglas defended his doctrine of popular sovereignty, insisting that each new state had the right to decide the question of slavery for itself. Slavery wasn't simply a matter of states' rights, Lincoln replied. It was a "vast moral evil," which affected all Americans—an evil that must be confined to the South, where it could be put on "the high road to extinction."

The candidates had agreed to hold seven three-hour debates, mostly in small Illinois towns. Thousands of people flocked to these events, coming from miles around aboard chartered trains and Illinois River boats, in wagons and buggies, on horseback and on foot, sitting or standing outdoors for hours under the summer sun, shouting questions, cheering or groaning or booing as the candidates went at it—debating the future of slavery in America. Skilled shorthand experts recorded every word of their speeches along with crowd reactions, while reporters telegraphed their stories to newspapers across the country.

The reporters noted how sharply the candidates differed in appearance as well as opinions. Douglas—five feet four inches tall, with a huge round head and a booming voice—came up only to Lincoln's shoulder. Reporters dubbed him "the Little Giant." Lincoln, exceptionally tall and painfully thin, towered above his stout opponent at six feet four. He was nicknamed "Long Abe."

Douglas pressed the issue of white supremacy. He warned white crowds that his opponent was a "black Republican" who wanted to liberate the slaves so they could stampede into Illinois to compete with white workers for jobs, to vote, and to marry white people. He claimed that Frederick Douglass, the black abolitionist, was one of Lincoln's closest advisers, even though Lincoln and Douglass had never laid eyes on each other. And he hammered away at his charge that Lincoln favored outright abolition. "I found Lincoln's ally in the person of Fred Douglass,

THE NEGRO, preaching abolition doctrines, when Lincoln was discussing the same principles," Senator Douglas charged.

Was Lincoln in favor of making Negroes the social and political equals of white people? Senator Douglas demanded. Did he favor a mixing of the races?

"The Little Giant" vs. "Long Abe": Lincoln and Douglas debate, 1858.

John Brown.

In a state like Illinois, where most voters opposed equal rights for blacks, these were touchy questions. Negro equality was not the issue, Lincoln protested. "I am not nor ever have been in favor of making voters or jurors of Negroes, nor of qualifying them to hold office, nor to intermarry with white people."

The real issue, Lincoln insisted, was "the difference between the men who think slavery a wrong and those who do not think it wrong." "That is the issue that will continue in this country when these poor tongues of Judge Douglas and myself shall be silent," he added. "It is the eternal struggle between these two principles—right and wrong—throughout the world."

At the time, U.S. senators were elected by state legislatures, not by popular vote. As it turned out, Douglas won reelection to the U.S. Senate for another six years. Lincoln was defeated. He was disappointed, but he felt that he had helped advance the cause of civil liberty. "The fight must go on," he told a friend. "The cause of civil liberty must not be surrendered at the end on *one*, or even, *one hundred* defeats."

* * *

On the evening of October 16, 1859, a militant abolitionist named John Brown, hoping to inspire a slave uprising, led a band of twenty-one men on a raid of the federal arsenal at Harpers Ferry, Virginia. Brown and his comrades gained control of the arsenal, but the slave rebellion never materialized. During a battle with federal troops, several of Brown's followers were killed. Brown himself was wounded and captured. When authorities searched his carpetbag, they found a letter from Frederick Douglass.

The two men had met years earlier and had remained friendly. Brown, in fact, had urged Douglass to join him in his assault on Harpers Ferry. While Douglass admired Brown's courage, he opposed his plan, and he urged Brown to call the raid off. He warned that Brown "was going into a perfect steel trap, and that once in, he would never get out alive."

Douglass played no part in the raid. And while the letter found in Brown's carpetbag was two years old and said nothing whatsoever about Harpers Ferry, it was evidence enough for the governor of Virginia to target Douglass as a fellow conspirator and charge him with "murder, robbery, and inciting servile insurrection in the State of Virginia."

A warrant was issued for Douglass's arrest. If captured, he

Harpers Ferry, 1859. A scene inside the engine house of the arsenal just before federal troops broke down the door, rescued the hostages standing against the wall, and captured John Brown. From Frank Leslie's Illustrated Newspaper, *November 5, 1859.*

would be sent to Virginia for trial; if convicted, he would be executed. For the second time in his life, Douglass fled the United States, going first to Canada and then to England. Brown, meanwhile, tried and convicted of murder and treason, was promptly hanged—becoming a martyr for countless Northerners who hated slavery. "All over the North men were singing the John Brown song," Douglass wrote. "His body was in the dust, but his soul was marching on."

Eventually, after excitement over the failed insurrection had died down, the charges against Douglass were dropped. He was able to return to the United States in time to take part in the presidential election of 1860. Lincoln had continued to speak out on the issues dividing the nation, and in May of that year he was nominated as the presidential candidate of the antislavery Republican Party.

1860 election poster.

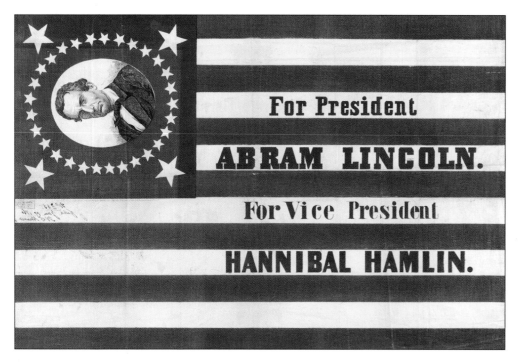

Lincoln faced a Democratic Party that had split into opposing factions. Northern Democrats nominated Illinois senator Stephen Douglas for president. Southern Democrats, unwilling to accept any Northerner, nominated John C. Breckinridge of Kentucky. Another group, the Constitutional Union Party, refused to join either the Democrats or Republicans and named John Bell of Tennessee as their candidate.

Frederick Douglass, safely back in Rochester, had mixed feelings about the election. He

Presidential candidates Lincoln and Douglas race toward Washington, D.C., in this political cartoon.

had been impressed with Lincoln during his debates with Stephen Douglas, calling Lincoln "a man of will and nerve, [who] will not back down from his own assertions," and a candidate who was "fully committed to the doctrine" of an unavoidable conflict between freedom and slavery.

However, Frederick Douglass was a dedicated abolitionist, while Lincoln insisted that he was not. Douglass had been one of the founders of the Radical Abolition Party, which demanded an *immediate end* to slavery everywhere. Lincoln and the Republicans opposed the *expansion* of slavery but believed that the Constitution protected slavery in the Southern states.

The Radical Abolitionists had nominated their own presidential candidate, Gerrit Smith, although they knew that Smith had no chance to be elected. Their goal was to stir up public interest in their cause and push the Republicans to take a more aggressive antislavery stand.

Douglass endorsed Smith, a longtime friend and supporter, as a matter of principle. He told readers of his newspaper that "ten thousand votes for Gerrit Smith . . . would do more than two million for ABRAHAM LINCOLN or any other" Republican. But he knew that Smith had no hope of winning, and when Lincoln was nominated, Douglass enthusiastically predicted that he would be elected president. He believed that a Republican victory would be a major advance in the battle against slavery.

"Abolitionist though I am," said Douglass, "and resolved to cast my vote for an abolitionist, I sincerely hope for the triumph of the Republican party against all the odds and ends of slavery combined against it."

He hoped the Republicans would win. But he told his friend Gerrit Smith, "I cannot support Lincoln."

The Democratic split helped sweep Abraham Lincoln into the White House. Lincoln carried every Northern state, receiving 1,866,000 votes to Douglas's 1,377,000 votes and Breckinridge's 850,000. John Bell of the new Constitutional Union Party received 589,000 votes. And the Radical Abolitionists, headed by Gerrit Smith, polled fewer than a thousand votes.

Lincoln's name did not even appear on the ballot in the South. Southern leaders had vowed that they would never accept this

Jefferson Davis, president of the Confederate States of America.

"Black Republican" as president. By the time Lincoln took his oath of office as president of the United States on March 4, 1861, seven Southern states had seceded from the Union, four more were about to join them, and Senator Jefferson Davis of Mississippi had been sworn in as president of the Confederate States of America.

With the Union collapsing, the Confederate states were preparing for a war of the North against the South.

Bombarding Fort Sumter: the shots that started the Civil War.
From an 1861 print.

— SEVEN —

Emancipation

The American Civil War began on the morning of April 12, 1861. At four thirty a.m., rebel cannons ringing the harbor at Charleston, South Carolina, opened fire on the American flag snapping in the sea breeze above the high brick walls of Fort Sumter. The Confederate states had declared themselves an independent nation. They demanded that the United States surrender all military fortifications within the boundaries of the South.

President Lincoln had pledged to "hold, occupy, and possess" all U.S. government forts and arsenals in the rebellious South. The garrison at Fort Sumter held out for thirty-three hours before being forced to surrender. On April 14, the American flag was hauled down and the Confederate stars and bars rose over the shattered and smoldering fort.

Lincoln, in office for little more than six weeks, issued a proclamation calling for 75,000 troops to put down the Southern rebellion. All over the North, patriotic crowds turned out to attend war rallies and cheer the flag. "I never knew what a popular excitement can be," reported a Harvard professor who had been born during the presidency of George Washington. "The whole population, men, women, and children seem to be in the streets with Union [souvenirs] and flags."

Senator Stephen Douglas, once Lincoln's archrival, now offered his support and called for national unity. "There are only two sides to the question," he told a mass meeting in Chicago. "Every man must be for the United States or against it. There can be no neutrals in this war, *only patriots—or traitors.*"

"God be praised!" Frederick Douglass exclaimed. The war "has come at last," and with it, the chance to destroy slavery. "Let the long crushed bondsman arise! and in this auspicious moment snatch back [his] liberty."

Douglass had great expectations, but he would be disappointed. He soon learned that he and President Lincoln had very different ideas about why the war was being fought and how it could be won.

Douglass saw the war as a chance to destroy slavery forever. He wanted Lincoln to free the slaves and recruit black soldiers into the Union army. Enslaved blacks were eager to cast off their chains and fight for their own freedom. Thousands of blacks were already escaping from behind Southern lines, ready to join the Union forces. "Every slave who escapes from the Rebel States is a loss to the Rebellion and a gain to the Loyal Cause," Douglass wrote. By arming only white men, he argued, the North was fighting the rebels with only one hand—"their soft white hand, while [keeping] their black iron hand chained and helpless behind them."

In Lincoln's view, this was a war to save the Union, not to destroy slavery. "We didn't go into the war to put down slavery," he said, "but to put the flag back." He was willing to leave slavery alone so long as it did not spread beyond the Southern states. Once the rebellion was crushed, slavery would be confined to the South, where, Lincoln still hoped and believed, it would gradually die out.

Lincoln worried that if he freed the slaves and enlisted black soldiers, he would alienate the large number of white Northerners who supported the Union but opposed emancipation. And

A party of escaped slaves coming into Union lines. Drawing by Edwin Forbes, 1863.

he feared that he would lose the support of the slaveholding border states—Delaware, Maryland, Kentucky, and Missouri—which had remained loyal to the Union. Without those loyal border states, Lincoln was convinced, the North could never win the war.

At first everyone in Washington, D.C., expected that the war would end quickly. The North claimed the loyalty of twenty-three states with a population of twenty-two million. It had factories to manufacture guns and ammunition, a network of railroads to transport troops, and a powerful navy to blockade Southern ports. The eleven Confederate states of the agricultural South had about nine million people. Nearly four million of them were slaves—a source of power, Frederick Douglass insisted, that could aid the Union cause.

Meanwhile the fighting dragged on without a decisive victory, and as the casualties mounted, so did criticism of President Lincoln. He had trouble finding field commanders he could count on and a reliable general in chief to direct the war effort. Most Republicans had come to agree with Frederick Douglass that saving the Union required freeing the slaves. They were demanding that the president come up with an emancipation policy.

"Free every slave—slay every traitor—burn every rebel mansion, if these things be necessary to preserve this temple of freedom," cried the Pennsylvania Republican congressman Thaddeus Stevens. "[We must] treat [this war] as a radical revolution and remodel our institutions."

Lincoln wasn't prepared to go quite that far—not yet. Instead, he supported a voluntary plan that would free the slaves gradually and compensate their owners, beginning with the loyal border states and extending into the South as each rebel state was conquered. But that plan went nowhere. Border-state

Before and after (opposite) photographs of a young escaped slave who became a Union drummer boy.

congressmen were not willing to accept even gradual, compensated emancipation.

And even if the slaves were liberated, would they be accepted as free and equal citizens of the United States? At first Lincoln doubted that freed slaves could overcome the nation's widespread racial prejudice. Perhaps they could be resettled in some distant colony, where they would not be subjected to humiliating discrimination and racial prejudice.

Lincoln actually suggested such a plan in August 1862, when he met at the White House with a delegation of five African Americans, most of them local clergymen, and urged them to consider emigrating to Central America. "We have between us a broader difference than exists between almost any other two races," he told them. "Your race are suffering, in my judgment, the greatest wrong inflicted on any people. But even when you cease to be slaves, you are yet far removed from being placed on an equality with the white race. You are cut off from many of the advantages which the other race enjoy." Perhaps, he concluded, "it is better for both of us to be separated."

Most American blacks scoffed at the idea of colonization. And Frederick Douglass was outraged when he read reports of the meeting. Lincoln's remarks, he charged, exposed his "pride of race and blood, his contempt for Negroes, and his canting hypocrisy." He pointed out that in Central and South America, "distinct races live peacefully together in the enjoyment of equal rights," without civil wars. And he called Lincoln "a genuine representative of American prejudice," who was more concerned about the border states than any principle of "justice and humanity."

Douglass understood the tough decisions the president faced and the resistance to emancipation by white Northerners who feared an invasion of liberated and jobless blacks. But he had expected more of Lincoln. He wasn't aware that the president had been listening to all the criticism, brooding over slavery, and wrestling with the idea of emancipation. Douglass didn't know it, but Lincoln had, in fact, been working on a preliminary draft of an Emancipation Proclamation that he had not made public.

Lincoln wanted to free the slaves, but he felt that the nation was not yet ready to support an antislavery war. He had maintained popular support for the war with its mounting death toll by insisting that his only goal was to restore the Union. His widely publicized White House meeting with a few black leaders was an effort to test public opinion and to make the idea of emancipation seem less threatening to Northern whites. "I can only go just as fast as I can see how to go," Lincoln said.

Powerful Republican senators had been pressing the president to act. Destroying slavery, they told him, was the quickest way to end the war. Slave labor was crucial to the South's war effort. Slaves grew the food that fed the Confederate army. They built the rebel army's fortifications. By freeing the slaves, Lincoln could cripple the Confederacy. By enlisting liberated slaves into the Union army, he could hasten the end of the war. "You need more men," Senator Charles Sumner told Lincoln, "not only at the North, but at the South, in the rear of the Rebels; you need the slaves."

Still, Lincoln hesitated. Did he, as president, have the authority to abolish slavery in those states where it was protected by law? His Republican advisers argued that under the war powers clause of the Constitution, the president, as commander in chief of the armed forces during an armed rebellion, had the right to emancipate the slaves. The Constitution gave the president powers in wartime that he did not have in peacetime. Emancipation during an armed rebellion was justified as a "fit and necessary war measure." Congress had already invoked the war powers clause to pass two laws confiscating the slaves of rebel owners.

Lincoln was ready to take the next step, but he wasn't convinced that public opinion was ready to follow. The war was not going well. Union troops had won no clear military victories in the critical eastern theater. Lincoln's secretary of state, William H. Seward, urged the president to wait—he must keep his Emancipation Proclamation under wraps until the Union had won a decisive victory in the east. Seward advised Lincoln to withhold publication of the proclamation until a military victory made

Lincoln reads the first draft of his Emancipation Proclamation to members of his cabinet, July 22, 1862. From an 1866 painting by F. B. Carpenter.

emancipation look like a demonstration of Northern strength rather than an act of desperation. To announce the proclamation now, Seward argued, would seem like a last-ditch attempt to cover up the Union's military blunders.

Lincoln agreed. His proclamation would be postponed until he could issue it from a position of strength. He was willing to wait until public opinion caught up with him. "It would do no good to go ahead any faster than the country would follow," he said.

On September 17, 1862, in the bloodiest single engagement of the war, Union troops under General George McClellan defeated Robert E. Lee's Confederate army at Antietam Creek in Maryland. It wasn't the decisive victory Lincoln hoped for—McClellan failed to pursue Lee as the rebels retreated back to Virginia—but it was good enough. The South's attempt to invade the North had been turned back.

On September 22, Lincoln read the final wording of his Emancipation Proclamation to his cabinet. The next day the document was released to the press. Issued as an "act of justice, warranted by the Constitution, upon military necessity," the proclamation declared that all slaves in rebel states that had not returned to the Union by January 1, 1863, "are and henceforward shall be free." In the loyal border states, Lincoln would continue to push for gradual, compensated emancipation.

"We shout for joy that we live to record this righteous decree," Frederick Douglass exclaimed. His hopes for the nation were suddenly revived. He regarded the proclamation as a revolutionary document that would lead to the end of slavery everywhere in America. "Slavery once abolished in the rebel states will give the death wound to slavery in the border states," he wrote. "Abraham Lincoln, in his own peculiar, cautious, forbearing and hesitating way, slow, but we hope sure, has . . . proclaimed and

declared" that as of January 1, the slaves in the rebellious South "Shall be Forever Free."

Douglass had criticized Lincoln harshly in the past, and he knew he would disagree with the president on many issues in the future. But with the Emancipation Proclamation, Frederick Douglass's attitude changed. He became an admirer of Abraham Lincoln.

Douglass recognized that no one individual, simply with a stroke of his pen, could emancipate four million enslaved human beings. Every day during the war, slaves had thrown off their shackles, fled from their masters, and escaped from behind Southern lines to fight for their own freedom. Black and white

Battle of Antietam, September 17, 1862. Five days later, Lincoln read the final wording of his Emancipation Proclamation to his cabinet. The Proclamation was made public the next day. From a painting by Christian Schussele.

abolitionists had worked together for years in their struggle to extinguish slavery. It was this long, continuing struggle, this background of resistance and courage and determination, that had led to the Emancipation Proclamation. "I claim not to have controlled events," Lincoln said, "but confess plainly that events have controlled me."

On New Year's Day, 1863, Lincoln slipped away from the holiday reception at the White House and retired to his office with his cabinet members and other officials to sign the proclamation that would make emancipation a reality. "I never in my life felt more certain that I was doing right, than I do in signing this paper," he said.

That evening in Boston, Frederick Douglass attended a celebration of black and white abolitionists at Tremont Temple. There were speeches, music, and presentations as everyone waited for official word from the nation's capital that Lincoln had signed the Emancipation Proclamation.

Watch meeting, December 31, 1862. African American men, women, and children gather around a man with a watch, waiting for the Emancipation Proclamation to take effect on January 1, 1863. This is from a carte de visite—a photographic print mounted on a small card. These cards, extremely popular in the early days of photography, were collected and traded throughout the world.

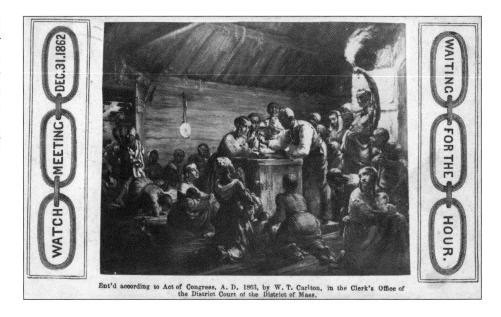

Freed slaves spread news of the emancipation.

By eleven p.m. word had not yet arrived. "We won't go home until morning," Douglass declared. Just then, a messenger burst into the hall, shouting, "It's coming! It is on the [telegraph] wires!"

The crowd erupted into cheers. People hugged one another and wept. "I never saw such enthusiasm before," Douglass said. "I never saw joy before. We give three cheers for Abraham Lincoln and three cheers for almost everybody else."

An estimated 200,000 black soldiers and sailors fought for the North during the Civil War.

~ EIGHT ~

"Mr. Douglass . . . I Am Glad to See You"

When the first rebel shots were fired at Fort Sumter, African Americans across the North volunteered to join the Union army. They were turned away by prejudice and federal law. Black soldiers had fought bravely in the American Revolution, but a decade later, in 1792, Congress passed the Militia Act, which barred blacks from serving in the army.

Frederick Douglass and other black leaders argued that by rejecting black soldiers, the North was undermining its war effort. But Northern voters and politicians opposed the use of black troops. And many white soldiers in the Union army did not want to fight alongside blacks. President Lincoln feared that enlisting blacks "would turn 50,000 bayonets from the loyal Border States against us that [previously] were for us." But even as he said that, he was beginning to change his mind.

As the war continued with no end in sight, public opinion also began to

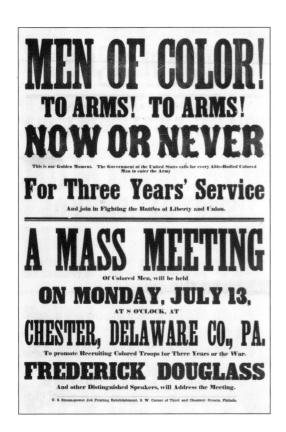

Recruiting poster. (Library Company of Philadelphia)

change. Northerners came to realize that it made sense to enlist blacks in a war for their own emancipation. Black troops could help crush the slaveholders' rebellion. A year after the Civil War began, Congress repealed the discriminatory clause of the 1792 Militia Act. The president could now enlist as many black soldiers as he thought necessary to put down the Southern rebellion.

When Lincoln announced in September 1862 that he planned to issue an Emancipation Proclamation, he ordered the War Department to start recruiting black soldiers. And when the final Proclamation was released on January 1, 1863, it included a provision authorizing the enlistment of blacks in the Union army.

Frederick Douglass joined other black leaders in calling for volunteers. He told black audiences that it was their moral obligation to fight for the Union. "Young men of Philadelphia, you are without excuse," he said in one speech. "The hour has arrived, and your place is in the Union army."

Among the first recruits whom Douglass signed up were two of his sons, eighteen-year-old Charles and twenty-year-old Lewis. They both joined the Fifty-fourth Massachusetts Volunteer Infantry, the nation's first black regiment from a free state. Lewis became the regiment's sergeant major, while Charles signed up as a private.

Black soldiers received about half the pay that whites did—they were paid as laborers (seven dollars a month) and not as soldiers (thirteen dollars a month). They had little chance of being promoted to the officer corps. Worse still, the South refused to treat captured black soldiers as prisoners of war; instead, Confederate soldiers executed their black prisoners or enslaved them.

Even so, black soldiers quickly proved their courage in widely reported battles at Port Huron in Louisiana and at Millikin's Bend on the Mississippi River north of Vicksburg. "The bravery of the blacks in the battle of Millikin's Bend completely revolutionized the sentiment of the army with regard to the employment of negro troops," reported Charles Dana, the assistant secretary of war.

Douglass's two sons took part in the Fifty-fourth Massachusetts regiment's assault on Fort Wagner, at the entrance to Charleston Harbor, where the Civil War had begun. On July 18, 1863, the Fifty-fourth attacked the fort, advancing across a narrow

Douglass's sons, twenty-year-old Lewis and eighteen-year-old Charles, were among the first black recruits to sign up. They joined the famous Fifty-fourth Massachusetts Volunteer Infantry, an all-black regiment commanded, like all such units, by white officers.

spit of sand in the face of fierce Confederate fire. Members of the regiment scaled the walls of the fort but after brutal hand-to-hand combat were driven out, suffering heavy casualties. Lewis Douglass was wounded during the fighting. The *New York Tribune* reported that this battle "made Fort Wagner such a name to the colored race as Bunker Hill had been for ninety years to the white Yankees."

"By arming the Negro we have added a powerful ally," General Ulysses Grant told Lincoln. "This, with the emancipation of the Negro, is the heaviest blow yet given the Confederacy."

All along, Douglass had been protesting in his speeches and newspaper articles the injustices inflicted on black soldiers. He called on the Lincoln administration to retaliate against the South's abuse of black prisoners. And on July 30 Lincoln issued an Order of Retaliation. For every captured Union soldier killed by the Confederacy, a rebel soldier would be executed. And for every Union soldier enslaved or sold into slavery by the Confederates, a rebel soldier would be placed at hard labor until the Union soldier was released and treated fairly as a prisoner of war.

Douglass was encouraged by Lincoln's action, but he wasn't satisfied. Why had it taken so long to issue the Retaliation Order? Why wasn't Lincoln doing something about the discrimination in pay and promotions suffered by black soldiers? Douglass decided "to go to Washington and lay the complaints of my people before President Lincoln," whom he had never met.

He rode the overnight train from Rochester to Washington, D.C. Arriving in the nation's capital on the muggy morning of August 10, 1863, he met Samuel C. Pomeroy, an antislavery senator from Kansas, who had offered to serve as Douglass's escort. Together they went to the War Department, where Douglass called on Edwin M. Stanton, the secretary of war.

The men of the Fifty-fourth demonstrated their courage when they stormed the walls of Fort Wagner in South Carolina on July 18, 1863. More than half the troops were killed or wounded, including their commander, Colonel Robert Gould Shaw, who was shot through the heart. From an 1890 lithograph.

Stanton's "manner was cold and businesslike throughout but earnest," Douglass recalled. They talked for half an hour. Douglass raised the issues of unequal pay for black troops and the lack of promotion opportunities. "Regulations confine them to the dead level of privates or noncommissioned officers," he complained. Even so, while pay and promotions were important, Douglass

Secretary of War Edwin M. Stanton.
He supported equal treatment for all soldiers.

said, black soldiers were fighting for "a cause quite independent of pay or place": they wanted freedom for their race and equality as American citizens.

Stanton brought up the "difficulties and prejudices to be surmounted" before black soldiers could achieve equality. But he told Douglass that he supported equal treatment for all soldiers. He believed in promotion by merit, he said, and he pledged to promote into officer ranks any black soldier recommended by his superior officer.

Leaving the War Department, Douglass and Pomeroy walked to the White House, where Douglass hoped to meet with President Lincoln. Handing his calling card to a clerk, he found a place on the stairway leading to Lincoln's office and sat down, prepared to wait.

"The stairway was crowded with applicants," he recalled. "Some of them looked eager; and I have no doubt some of them had a purpose in being there, and wanted to see the President for the good of the country! They were white; and as I was the only dark spot among them, I expected to have to wait at least half a day; I had heard of men waiting a week."

Within minutes, however, one of Lincoln's assistants appeared and called out, "Mr. Douglass!" As Douglass was escorted up the crowded stairway, "pressing and elbowing my way through," he heard someone grumble, "Yes, damn it! I knew they would let the nigger through."

Douglass was ushered into the president's simply furnished office. Books and papers were strewn about everywhere. Lincoln was seated in a low armchair, his long legs reaching into "different parts of the room."

As Douglass entered, "the President began to rise, and he continued rising until he stood over me." Both men were unusually tall for their time, but Lincoln rose above Douglass by a good three inches. He reached out to shake Douglass's hand. "Mr. Douglass, I know you," he said. "I have read about you, and Mr. Seward [the secretary of state] has told me about you. . . . Sit down, I am glad to see you."

Douglass had criticized Lincoln severely in the past, and he wasn't sure how he might be received. The president's friendly manner quickly put him at ease. With "an earnestness and a fluency which I had not expected," Lincoln defended his wartime policies. His critics claimed that he took too long to make decisions. They had attacked him for being "tardy" and "hesitating" about emancipation and enlisting black troops. Lincoln acknowledged that at times he might be slow to act. He had hesitated to push for certain policies when he believed that "the country was not yet ready." But once he had taken a position, he insisted, "I have never retreated from it."

Lincoln's Order of Retaliation for the Confederate abuse of black prisoners was an example. "The country needed talking up to on that point," he said. Had he issued the order any sooner, "such was the state of popular prejudice that an outcry would have been raised against the measure."

"Remember this, Mr. Douglass," Lincoln added. Recent battles in which black soldiers had distinguished themselves for bravery "were necessary to prepare the way" for the policy of retaliation.

As Douglass recalled the conversation, Lincoln wasn't really comfortable with that policy—"a terrible remedy, very difficult to apply." He had no problem retaliating against a Confederate soldier who was guilty of murdering or enslaving a black prisoner. But the policy of executing a man for a crime committed by someone else was hard for Lincoln to accept, and while the policy might be necessary, he was reluctant to enforce it.

As Douglass listened to the president speak, he "saw the tender heart of the man rather than the stern warrior . . . and while I could not agree with him, I could but respect his humane spirit."

When Douglass raised the issue of unequal pay, Lincoln promised that black soldiers would eventually receive the same pay as white soldiers. And he pledged to sign any promotions for black soldiers that the secretary of war recommended.

Douglass came away from the meeting elated. He had been totally charmed by Lincoln's "transparent countenance," by his honesty and sincerity, by "the patience and silence" with which

The hanged body of William Johnson, a black Union soldier. Black prisoners of war were executed or enslaved by their Confederate captors.

the president had listened "to all I had to say," and by the courtesy he had accorded a longtime critic. "There was no vain pomp and ceremony about him," Douglass wrote. "I was never in any way reminded of my humble origin, or of my unpopular color." Douglass sensed that Lincoln was someone "whom I could love, honor, and trust without reserve or doubt."

The admiration was mutual. Not long afterward, Lincoln told a friend that he regarded Douglass as "one of the most meritorious men in America."

"Mr. Douglass, never come to Washington without calling upon me," Lincoln told him in parting.

Ward in a military hospital, Washington, D.C., 1864.
Mosquito nets hang over the beds. Total Civil War casualties
exceeded the nation's loss in all other wars, from the
Revolution to the present.

∼ NINE ∼

Lincoln's Secret Plan

"We are in the midst of strange and terrible times," exclaimed the poet Walt Whitman. The war news was indeed terrible. In May 1864 the armies of generals Grant and Lee clashed in a heavily wooded area of Virginia called the Wilderness and fought to a standstill, with heavy casualties on both sides. During a single week Grant alone lost 32,000 men killed, wounded, and missing.

In July, Confederate troops crossed the Potomac. In a daring raid on Washington, they cut the capital's telegraph lines and came within five miles of the White House.

Ambulances streaming in from the battlefields caused traffic jams on Washington streets. "When This Cruel War Is Over" was the year's most popular song. People everywhere were clamoring for peace. Many Northerners were convinced that Lincoln's antislavery policy was the stumbling block that prevented a peaceful settlement with the Confederate states.

"Our bleeding, bankrupt, almost dying country longs for peace," newspaper publisher Horace Greeley told the president. "I entreat you to submit overtures for [peace] to the Southern insurgents."

Lincoln was facing reelection in November, and he felt certain that he would lose. "I am going to be beaten," he said, "and unless some great change takes place *badly* beaten."

Antiwar Democrats, demanding peace at any price, were determined to turn the president out of office. And some leading Republicans, members of Lincoln's own party, were threatening to abandon him and support another nominee for president. They charged that Lincoln was bungling the war effort, that he would be too lenient with the South when the war was over, and that in any case he was too unpopular to win reelection.

"The tide is setting strongly against us," Henry J. Raymond, chairman of the Republican National Committee, told the president. He attributed the backlash against Lincoln to "two special causes . . . the want of military success" and "the impression in some minds, the fear and suspicion in others" that Lincoln was "fighting not for the Union but for the abolition of slavery."

Despite opposition, Lincoln held fast to his conviction that the Union could not be restored without emancipating the slaves. Some 130,000 black soldiers and sailors were now fighting for the Union. By the end of the war, 180,000 black soldiers, one Union soldier in ten, and 20,000 black sailors would be fighting for the North. "If they stake their lives for us," Lincoln said, "they must be prompted by the strongest motive—even the promise of freedom. And the promise being made, must be kept."

To abandon the goal of emancipation, Lincoln believed, "would ruin the Union cause. . . . All colored men now in our service would instantly desert us. And rightfully too. Why should they give their lives for us, with full notice of our purpose to betray them? . . . Abandon all the [military] posts now possessed by black men, surrender all these advantages to the enemy, & we would be compelled to abandon the war in 3 weeks."

How, Lincoln asked, could he "return to slavery the black warriors" who had fought for the Union? "I should be damned in time & in eternity for so doing. The world shall know that I shall keep my faith to friends & enemies, come what will."

Lincoln was still convinced that "the emancipation policy and the use of colored troops constitute the heaviest blow yet dealt to the rebellion." He worried that if he lost the election, his successor would negotiate a peace restoring the Union and leaving countless blacks still in bondage.

Black soldiers had helped the Union army win crucial victories. Perhaps blacks could now play another role. Lincoln had an idea—a secret plan. And he needed Frederick Douglass to help carry it out. He invited Douglass back to the White House for a second meeting.

Douglass had started to criticize the president again. He complained that Lincoln was still reluctant to retaliate when captured black soldiers were executed or enslaved. And he charged that the president was ignoring the issue of black voting rights. Blacks were good enough to fight for the government, Douglass told a friend, but not good enough to vote for the government. Even so, he welcomed the chance to return to the White House and air his grievances in another face-to-face meeting. "I need not say I went most gladly," he wrote.

This time, a White House messenger was waiting to greet Douglass as he stepped off his train on the morning of August 18.

When Douglass was ushered into Lincoln's office, he found the president "in an alarmed condition." Lincoln was concerned about Northern opposition to the war and worried about his reelection chances. If he was voted out of office, his successor could offer the rebels peace terms that would restore the Union but leave slavery in place where it still existed.

Hundreds of thousands of slaves had already won freedom for themselves by escaping to Union lines. But millions more remained enslaved on farms and plantations throughout the Confederate South. "The slaves are not coming so rapidly and so numerously as I had hoped," Lincoln told Douglass.

They might not have heard about the Emancipation Proclamation, Douglass suggested. Masters "knew how to keep such things from their slaves," he said. "Probably very few [slaves] knew of [the] proclamation."

Lincoln had a plan to bring more slaves into Union lines and freedom. He wanted Douglass to organize an elite band of black scouts "to go into the rebel states, beyond the lines of our armies, carry the news of emancipation, and urge the slaves to come within our boundaries."

Douglass listened "with the deepest interest and profoundest satisfaction" as Lincoln spoke and agreed to organize such a plan. His scouts would move through the South as agents of the U.S. government, spreading the word that the president had issued an Emancipation Proclamation and that freedom for all would be guaranteed by the invading Union army. If the plan worked, it would help bring the war to an end while liberating slaves. And to make sure that the slaves remained liberated, Lincoln wanted to pass a constitutional amendment abolishing slavery forever throughout the United States.

As they discussed the plan, a secretary interrupted to remind

Hundreds of thousands of slaves won freedom for themselves by escaping to Union lines. Illustration from Harper's Weekly, *February 21, 1863.*

Lincoln that the governor of Connecticut was waiting to see him. Douglass offered to step outside, but Lincoln objected. "Tell Governor Buckingham to wait," Lincoln said, "for I want to have a long talk with my friend Frederick Douglass." They continued talking, Douglass recalled, for "a full hour after this," while the governor waited.

The two men had much in common, and, it seems, they enjoyed each other's company. They had both come a long way, rising from poverty and obscurity. They had both educated themselves and in fact read many of the same books—as they may have discussed. And they shared a common purpose. Douglass needed Lincoln's help to rid the nation of slavery. Lincoln needed Douglass to help him end the war and reunite the nation.

Lincoln "treated me as a man," Douglass told a friend the next day. "He did not let me feel for a moment that there was any difference in the color of our skins. The president is a most remarkable man."

Douglass came away from the meeting with a changed view of Lincoln. He now saw in the president "a deeper moral conviction against slavery than I had ever seen before in anything spoken or written by him."

Douglass spent the next few days in Washington at a friend's house, writing a memo to the president detailing his plans to spread the word of emancipation throughout the rebel South. One afternoon a White House messenger arrived with an invitation from the president to join him for tea at the Old Soldiers Home, where Lincoln regularly went to relax. A carriage was waiting outside. A few days earlier, Douglass had gone to the White House to discuss urgent business. This invitation was social—a simple gesture of friendship. Regretfully, Douglass couldn't accept. He had agreed to deliver a lecture elsewhere in Washington that day.

He returned to Rochester prepared to carry out the president's plan. "Every slave who escapes from the rebel states is a loss to the rebellion and a gain to the loyal cause," he wrote to Lincoln. But before Douglass could recruit scouts to infiltrate the South, Lincoln's plan turned out to be unnecessary after all. As the presidential election approached, a succession of decisive Union victories signaled that the end of the war was in sight at last.

In Georgia, the city of Atlanta was captured after a long siege. With Atlanta in flames, General William T. Sherman's army set out on a devastating march across Georgia to the sea, smashing and burning everything in its path. In Virginia, General Philip H. Sheridan's cavalry troops were sweeping through the Shenandoah Valley, while General Grant was tightening his stranglehold on the Confederate capital at Richmond.

In the North, the public mood shifted dramatically. Lincoln's critics closed ranks around him. "All hesitation ought to cease," Douglass declared, "and every man who wishes well to the slave and to the country should at once rally with all the warmth and earnestness of his nature to the support of Abraham Lincoln."

Lincoln won a second term as president by nearly half a million votes. He took advantage of his victory to press forward with his emancipation program. As a wartime measure, a *military necessity*, the Emancipation Proclamation might be overturned by some future Congress or court. But a *constitutional amendment* would be "a King's cure for all the evils," as Lincoln put it. It

Battle of Atlanta, Georgia, July 22, 1864, as depicted by artist James E. Taylor.

President Lincoln enters the conquered Confederate capital of Richmond, Virginia, April 3, 1865. Engraving by John Chester Buttre, 1866.

would abolish slavery permanently, not just in the rebel South but everywhere in America.

Lincoln urged Congress to approve such a measure. The final vote came on January 31, 1865, when a cheering House of Representatives passed and sent to the states for ratification the Thirteenth Amendment to the Constitution, permanently abolishing slavery throughout the United States.

As the House clerk read out the results of the vote—119 for the amendment, 56 opposed—elated congressmen jumped around in the aisles, embraced one another, and "wept like children," while shouts and applause broke out in the gallery. Among the spectators who witnessed the vote from the gallery that historic day, cheering and weeping for joy, were many black people. Their presence was testimony to the revolutionary changes taking place, for until 1864, just a year earlier, blacks had not been allowed in congressional galleries.

Telegraph wires carried the news across the nation, and that evening African Americans gathered in mass meetings to clap and sing and rejoice:

> *Sound the loud timbrel o'er Egypt's dark sea,*
> *Jehovah has triumphed, his people are free.*

Scene in the U.S. House of Representatives following the passage of the Thirteenth Amendment, permanently abolishing slavery in the United States.

*Abraham Lincoln delivers his second inaugural address
in front of the U.S. Capitol, March 4, 1865.*

— TEN —

"My Friend Douglass"

On the morning of March 4, 1865, Frederick Douglass joined a festive crowd of 30,000 spectators at the U.S. Capitol to witness Abraham Lincoln's second inauguration. Weeks of rain had turned Washington's unpaved streets into a sea of mud, but despite the wet and windy weather, the crowd was in a mood to celebrate. Union troops were marching victoriously through the South. Everyone knew that the war was almost over. When Lincoln's tall figure appeared, "cheer upon cheer arose, bands blatted upon the air, and flags waved all over the scene."

Douglass found a place for himself directly in front of the speaker's stand. He could see every crease in Lincoln's careworn face as the president stepped forward to deliver his second inaugural address.

The Civil War had cost more than 600,000 American lives. The fighting had been more bitter and lasted far longer than anyone could have imagined. The "cause of the war" was slavery, Lincoln declared. Slavery was the one institution that divided the nation. And slavery was a hateful and evil practice—a sin in the sight of God. "This mighty scourge of war" was a terrible retribution, a punishment for allowing human bondage to flourish on the nation's soil. Now that slavery was abolished, the time had come "to bind up the nation's wounds" and "cherish a just and lasting peace among ourselves and with all nations."

Following the "wonderfully quiet, earnest, and solemn" ceremony, Douglass wanted to congratulate Lincoln personally. That evening he joined the crowd heading to attend the gala inaugural reception at the White House—a building completed with slave labor just a half century earlier. "Though no colored persons had ever ventured to present themselves on such occasions," Douglass wrote, "it seemed, now that freedom had become the law of the republic, and colored men were on the battlefield, mingling their blood with that of white men in one common effort to save the country, that it was not too great an assumption for a colored man to offer his congratulations to the President with those of other citizens."

At the White House door, Douglass was stopped by two policemen who "took me rudely by the arm and ordered me to stand back." Their orders, they told him, were "to admit no persons of my color." Douglass didn't believe them. He was positive that no such order could have come from the president.

The police tried to steer Douglass away from the doorway and out a side exit. He refused to leave. "I shall not go out of this building till I see President Lincoln," he insisted. Just then he spotted an acquaintance who was entering the building and asked him to send word "to Mr. Lincoln that Frederick Douglass is detained

by officers at the door." Within moments, Douglass was being escorted into the elegant East Room of the White House.

Lincoln stood among his guests "like a mountain pine high above all others." As Douglass approached through the crowd, Lincoln called out, "Here comes my friend Douglass." The president took Douglass by the hand. "I am glad to see you," he said. "I saw you in the crowd today, listening to my inaugural address. How did you like it?"

The inaugural reception at the White House. Illustration from Frank Leslie's Chimney Corner, *1865.*

The last photograph taken of a careworn Abraham Lincoln before his assassination.

Douglass hesitated. "Mr. Lincoln, I must not detain you with my poor opinion, when there are thousands waiting to shake hands with you."

"No, no," said the president. "You must stop a little Douglass; there is no man whose opinion I value more than yours. I want to know what you think of it."

"Mr. Lincoln, that was a sacred effort," Douglass replied.

"I'm glad you liked it!"

And with that, Douglass moved on, making way for other guests who were waiting to shake the hand of Abraham Lincoln.

A month later, on April 9, 1865, generals Grant and Lee met at Appomattox Courthouse in Virginia, where Grant accepted the surrender of Lee's Confederate army. After almost four years of savage fighting, the Civil War had ended. "Guns are firing, bells ringing, flags flying, men laughing, children cheering, all, all jubilant," Gideon Welles, Lincoln's secretary of the navy, recorded in his diary.

Throngs of people collected around the White House, calling for the president. When Lincoln appeared, he asked the band to play "Dixie," a popular minstrel tune that had become associated with the Confederate cause. "It is one of the best tunes I have ever heard," Lincoln told the crowd. He joked that the tune was now "a lawful prize," since "we fairly captured it." So the band played "Dixie," then struck up "Yankee Doodle."

Five days later, as Lincoln sat watching a play with his wife at Ford's Theater in Washington, the president was shot in the head by actor John Wilkes Booth. Lincoln died early the next morning, April 15, 1865.

"A dreadful disaster has befallen the nation," Frederick Douglass told a memorial service in Rochester that afternoon. "It is a day for silence and meditation; for grief and tears."

For Douglass, Lincoln's death was "a personal as well as a national calamity." He felt that he had lost a friend, and how deeply he mourned that day for Abraham Lincoln, "I dare not attempt to tell. It was only a few days ago that I shook his brave, honest hand, and looked into his gentle eye and heard his kindly voice."

A few months later Douglass received in the mail a long, slender package from Washington, D.C., along with a note from Mary Todd Lincoln. Her husband had considered Douglass a special friend, she wrote, and before he died, he had wanted to do something to express his warm personal regard. Since he hadn't had the chance, Mary had decided to send Douglass her husband's favorite walking stick as a memento of their friendship.

* * *

When Abraham Lincoln was assassinated, Frederick Douglass, in his mid-forties, was America's most influential black citizen. For the rest of his long life, he continued in his speeches and writings to be a powerful voice for social justice, denouncing racism and demanding equal rights for blacks and whites alike. During the Reconstruction era of the 1870s and 1880s, when many of the rights gained after emancipation were snatched away in the South, Douglass spoke out against lynchings, the terrorism of the Ku Klux Klan, and the Jim Crow laws that were devised to keep blacks in their place and away from the ballot box.

As he traveled widely, lecturing on social issues and national politics, Douglass spoke often about Abraham Lincoln. During the war, he had criticized the president for being slow to move against slavery, for resisting the enlistment of black soldiers, for inviting blacks "to leave the land in which we were born." But with emancipation, and in the aftermath of the war, Douglass

Frederick Douglass, around 1879.

had come to appreciate Lincoln's sensitivity to popular opinion and to admire the political skills Lincoln employed to win public support. "His greatest mission was to accomplish two things: first, to save the country from dismemberment and ruin; and, second, to free his country from the great crime of slavery. To do one or the other, or both," Douglass said, Lincoln needed "the earnest sympathy and the powerful cooperation of his fellow countrymen."

In the 1870s, Douglass moved with his family to Washington,

Douglass in his library at Cedar Hill.

D.C., where he edited a newspaper, held a succession of federal appointments, and clearly enjoyed his exalted position as an elder statesman of America's black citizens. And he continued to denounce injustice and inequality with the undiminished fervor of an old warrior.

His last home was a large, comfortable house called Cedar Hill, perched high on a hilltop looking down at the Anacostia River and the U.S. capital beyond. Cedar Hill had a spacious library, large enough to hold Douglass's collection of some two thousand books. From time to time, as he picked a book from his shelves and settled down to read, he must have recalled those distant days in Baltimore when he was a young slave named Frederick Bailey, a determined boy who owned just one book, a single volume that he kept hidden from view and read in secret.

Lincoln had read and studied the same book as a young man in New Salem. That was something they had in common, a shared experience that helped each of them rise from obscurity to greatness. "He was the architect of his own fortune, a self-made man," Douglass wrote of Lincoln. He had "ascended high, but with hard hands and honest work built the ladder on which he climbed"—words that Douglass, as he was aware, could easily have applied to himself.

DIALOGUE BETWEEN A MASTER AND SLAVE.

Master. NOW, villain! what have you to say for this second attempt to run away? Is there any punishment that you do not deserve?

Slave. I well know that nothing I can say will avail. I submit to my fate.

Mast. But are you not a base fellow, a hardened and ungrateful rascal?

Slave. I am a slave. That is answer enough.

Mast. I am not content with that answer. I thought I discerned in you some tokens of a mind superiour to your condition. I treated you accordingly. You have been comfortably fed and lodged, not over-worked, and attended with the most humane care when you were sick. And is this the return?

Slave. Since you condescend to talk with me, as man to man, I will reply. What have you done, what can you do for me that will compensate for the liberty which you have taken away?

Mast. I did not take it away. You were a slave when I fairly purchased you.

Slave. Did I give my consent to the purchase?

Mast. You had no consent to give. You had already lost the right of disposing of yourself.

Slave. I had lost the power, but how the right? I was treacherously kidnapped in my own country, when following an honest occupation. I was put in chains, sold to one of your countrymen, carried by force on board his ship, brought hither, and exposed to sale like a beast in the market, where you bought me. What step in all this progress of violence and injustice can give a *right?* Was it in the villain who stole me, in the slave-merchant who tempted him to do so, or in you who encouraged the slave-merchant to bring his cargo of human cattle to cultivate your lands?

Mast.

THE COLUMBIAN ORATOR. 241

Mast. It is in the order of Providence that one man should become subservient to another. It ever has been so, and ever will be. I found the custom, and did not make it.

Slave. You cannot but be sensible, that the robber who puts a pistol to your breast may make just the same plea. Providence gives him a power over your life and property; it gave my enemies a power over my liberty. But it has also given me legs to escape with; and what should prevent me from using them? Nay, what should restrain me from retaliating the wrongs I have suffered, if a favourable occasion should offer?

Mast. Gratitude! I repeat, gratitude! Have I not endeavoured ever since I possessed you, to alleviate your misfortunes by kind treatment; and does that confer no obligation? Consider how much worse your condition might have been under another master.

Slave. You have done nothing for me more than for your working cattle. Are they not well fed and tended? do you work them harder than your slaves? is not the rule of treating both designed only for your own advantage? You treat both your men and beast slaves better than some of your neighbours, because you are more prudent and wealthy than they.

Mast. You might add, more humane too.

Slave. Humane! Does it deserve that appellation to keep your fellow-men in forced subjection, deprived of all exercise of their free will, liable to all the injuries that your own caprice, or the brutality of your overseers, may heap on them, and devoted, soul and body, only to your pleasure and emolument? Can gratitude take place between creatures in such a state, and the tyrant who holds them in it? Look at these limbs; are they not those of a man? Think that I have the spirit of a man too.

Mast. But it was my intention not only to make your life tolerably comfortable at present, but to provide for you in your old age.

W

Slave.

242 THE COLUMBIAN ORATOR.

Slave. Alas! is a life like mine, torn from country, friends, and all I held dear, and compelled to toil under the burning sun for a master, worth thinking about for old age? No: the sooner it ends, the sooner I shall obtain that relief for which my soul pants.

Mast. Is it impossible, then, to hold you by any ties but those of constraint and severity?

Slave. It is impossible to make one, who has felt the value of freedom, acquiesce in being a slave.

Mast. Suppose I were to restore you to your liberty, would you reckon that a favour?

Slave. The greatest; for although it would only be undoing a wrong, I know too well how few among mankind are capable of sacrificing interest to justice, not to prize the exertion when it is made.

Mast. I do it, then; be free.

Slave. Now I am indeed your servant, though not your slave. And as the first return I can make for your kindness, I will tell you freely the condition in which you live. You are surrounded with implacable foes, who long for a safe opportunity to revenge upon you and the other planters all the miseries they have endured. The more generous their natures, the more indignant they feel against that cruel injustice which has dragged them hither, and doomed them to perpetual servitude. You can rely on no kindness on your part, to soften the obduracy of their resentment. You have reduced them to the state of brute beasts; and if they have not the stupidity of beasts of burden, they must have the ferocity of beasts of prey. Superior force alone can give you security. As soon as that fails, you are at the mercy of the merciless. Such is the social bond between master and slave!

PART

Historic Sites

Frederick Douglass's last home, Cedar Hill, with its sweeping view of downtown Washington, D.C., has been preserved as the Frederick Douglass National Historic Site, administered by the National Park Service. Visitors to the fourteen-room house can see Douglass's personal belongings, home furnishings, and photographs of family and friends. The library, with its vast collection of books and the roll-top desk where Douglass wrote his final autobiography and many speeches, serves as a poignant reminder that he was self-taught and continued to read and learn throughout his life. The Visitor Center features a seventeen-minute film about his life, has exhibits and a bookshop, and sells tickets for a tour of the house. It is located at 1411 W Street SE, Washington, D.C. 20020, (202) 426-5961, www.nps.gov/frdo/index.htm.

National Historic Sites devoted to Abraham Lincoln include the Abraham Lincoln Birthplace National Historical Park, 2995 Lincoln Farm Road, Hodgenville, KY 42748, (270) 358-3137, www.nps.gov/abli/index.htm; the Lincoln Boyhood National Memorial, four miles west of Santa Claus, IN, on State Route 162, (812) 937-4541; the Lincoln Home National Historic Site, 413 South 8th Street, Springfield, IL 62701, (217) 492-4241, www.nps.gov/liho/index.htm; and the Ford's Theater National Historic Site, 511 10th Street NW, Washington, D.C. 20004, (202) 426-6924, www.nps.gov/foth/index.htm.

Selected Bibliography

When I was working on my book *Lincoln: A Photobiography* during the 1980s, Lincoln's brief but telling friendship with Frederick Douglass was not a subject that received a great deal of attention in the vast and ever-expanding Lincoln literature (by one estimate, 16,000 books have been published about Lincoln so far). Recent years have seen the emergence of a group of scholars who have examined in considerable depth the Lincoln-Douglass relationship and its consequences for the conduct of the Civil War and for race relations in America. I became aware of this view when I read Garry Wills's essay "Lincoln's Black History," in the June 11, 2009, issue of the *New York Review of Books.* That led me to John Stauffer's June 26, 2005, *Time* magazine essay, "Across the Great Divide," and to the following books that have advanced the study of Lincoln and emancipation by treating Frederick Douglass as an equal protagonist: James Oakes, *The Radical and the Republican: Frederick Douglass, Abraham Lincoln, and the Triumph of Antislavery Politics* (New York: W. W. Norton, 2007); and John Stauffer, *Giants: The Parallel Lives of Frederick Douglass and Abraham Lincoln* (New York: Twelve, 2008). The same story is explored in Paul Kendrick and Stephen Kendrick, *Douglass and Lincoln: How a Revolutionary Black Leader and a Reluctant Liberator Struggled to End Slavery and Save the Union* (New York: Walker and Company, 2007).

The richest sources on the life of Frederick Douglass are his three not-always-consistent autobiographies: *Narrative of the Life of Frederick Douglass, an American Slave: Written by Himself,* a classic of American autobiography (New York: Barnes & Noble

Classics, 2003; available in several editions and originally published in 1845 by the Boston Anti-Slavery Society); *My Bondage and My Freedom* (New York: Modern Library, 2003; originally published in 1855 in New York by Miller, Orton & Mulligan); and *Life and Times of Frederick Douglass, Written by Himself: His Early Life as a Slave, His Escape from Bondage, and His Complete History* (New York: Macmillan Company, 1962; first published in 1881 and revised in 1892).

The only full-length Douglass biography available at present is William S. McFeely's invaluable *Frederick Douglass* (New York: W. W. Norton, 1991). Dickson J. Preston's *Young Frederick Douglass: The Maryland Years* (Baltimore: Johns Hopkins University Press, 1980) explores Douglass's family roots and the society in which he came of age, from his birth on Maryland's East Shore in 1818 to his escape in 1838. Douglass's meetings with Lincoln are described in Benjamin Quarles's *Lincoln and the Negro* (New York: Oxford University Press, 1962), the first book to examine in any detail how Lincoln approached the status of black people in American democracy. And Caleb Bingham's *The Columbian Orator*, a book that influenced both Douglass and Lincoln, is available today as a facsimile copy of the original edition, first published in New York in 1816.

Among the innumerable Lincoln biographies, the definitive single-volume study for our times is David Herbert Donald's deeply researched *Lincoln* (New York: Simon & Schuster, 1995). I also returned to three previous modern standards: Stephen B. Oates's *With Malice Toward None: The Life of Abraham Lincoln* (New York: Harper & Row, 1977), Benjamin P. Thomas's *Abraham Lincoln: A Biography* (New York: Alfred A. Knopf, 1952), and Carl Sandburg's *Abraham Lincoln: The Prairie Years and the War Years*, one-volume edition (New York: Harcourt Brace Jovanovich, 1954; originally published in 1926 and 1939).

Finally, I am indebted to James M. McPherson's landmark work *Battle Cry of Freedom: The Civil War Era* (New York: Oxford University Press, 1988).

Notes

The following notes refer to the sources of quoted material. Each citation includes the first and last words of the quotation and the source or sources. Unless otherwise noted, all references are to works cited in the Selected Bibliography beginning on page 108.
   Abbreviations used:

Bingham: Caleb Bingham, *The Columbian Orator*
Bondage: Frederick Douglass, *My Bondage and My Freedom*
Donald: David Herbert Donald, *Lincoln*
Life & Times: Frederick Douglass, *Life and Times of Frederick Douglass*
McFeely: William S. McFeely, *Frederick Douglass*
McPherson: James M. McPherson, *Battle Cry of Freedom*
Narrative: Frederick Douglass, *Narrative of the Life of Frederick Douglass*
Oakes: James Oakes, *The Radical and the Republican*
Oates: Stephen B. Oates, *With Malice Toward None*
Sandburg: Carl Sandburg, *Abraham Lincoln*
Stauffer: John Stauffer, *Giants*
Thomas: Benjamin P. Thomas, *Abraham Lincoln*

1: Waiting for Mr. Lincoln

Page:

1 "public opinion baths": Thomas, p. 462
   "They do not . . . their place": Thomas, p. 457

2 "to secure . . . treatment": *Life & Times*, p. 346
   "lay the complaints . . . Lincoln": *Life & Times*, p. 346

3 "nerve": *Life & Times*, p. 346
   "The distance . . . altogether": *Life & Times*, p. 346

2: Born into Slavery

5 "I have no . . . ignorant": *Narrative*, p. 17
   "The white children . . . spirit": *Narrative*, p. 17

6 "My father . . . parentage": *Narrative*, p. 17

7 "She was . . . sunrise": *Narrative*, p. 18
   "The louder . . . my turn next": *Narrative*, pp. 20–21

7–8 "there would be . . . unhappy": *Narrative*, p. 41

8 "I now understood . . . how to read": *Narrative*, p. 41

9 "As many . . . to read": *Narrative*, p. 44

"You will be free . . . you have?": *Narrative*, p. 44

"I do not remember . . . system": McFeely, p. 34

"that gem . . . slavery": McFeely, p. 51

11 "The more I read . . . run away": *Narrative*, pp. 45–47

"cruel . . . ways": *Narrative*, p. 56

"unsuitable . . . broken": *Narrative*, pp. 57–58

"slave breaker . . . whipping": *Narrative*, p. 59

11–12 "We were worked . . . field": *Narrative*, pp. 62–63

12 "in a sort . . . fear": *Narrative*, p. 63

"with saddened . . . freedom": *Narrative*, pp. 63–64

"I resolved . . . at all": *Narrative*, pp. 68–69

12–13 "The only . . . unpunished": *Narrative*, p. 70

13 "My treatment . . . single blow": *Narrative*, pp. 74, 76

"we all denied . . . away": *Narrative*, p. 81

13–14 "to my surprise . . . might be killed": *Narrative*, p. 83

14 "In the course . . . caulkers": *Narrative*, p. 86

15 "I earned it . . . Master Hugh": *Narrative*, p. 87

"This arrangement . . . freeman": *Narrative*, p. 90

"only increased . . . freedom": *Narrative*, p. 87

17 "abolitionists . . . freedom": *Narrative*, p. 86

"If I failed . . . escape": *Narrative*, p. 92

3: Soul on Fire

20 "This was . . . round the world": *Life & Times*, p. 199

20–21 "But this . . . held his peace": *Life & Times*, p. 201

21 "it was . . . lions": *Narrative*, p. 93

"hurrying throng," "dazzling wonders": Bondage, p. 199

21 "I was yet . . . wrong one": *Narrative*, p. 93

22 "new . . . dress": McFeely, p. 33

"I shouldered . . . the other": *Narrative*, p. 95

"I was now . . . of it": *Narrative*, p. 98

24 "mastered": Stauffer, p. 79

"The paper . . . fire": *Narrative*, p. 99

25 "I could . . . by others": *Narrative*, p. 99

"say a few words": *Life & Times*, p. 215

"The truth . . . down": *Narrative*, p. 99

"It was . . . remember": *Life & Times*, p. 215

26 "that laughed . . . humor": McFeely, p. 100

"stood locked . . . against us": McFeely, p. 114

"*Notice!* . . . at 7 o'clock": *Life & Times*, p. 224

27–28 "Many persons . . . devise": Stauffer, p. 90

29 "the most . . . *important!*": Stauffer, p. 91

"spare no pains . . . South": Stauffer, p. 91

31 "All rights for all": Stauffer, p. 134

"Justice . . . be silent": McFeely, pp. 146–47

4: Nothing but Plenty of Friends

34 "the panther's . . . fear": Donald, p. 23

35 "did not . . . one year": Donald, p. 29

"It didn't . . . like that": Sandburg, p. 13

36 "He can sink . . . ever saw": Sandburg, p. 14

37 "The horrid . . . yet": Stauffer, p. 57

"a friendless . . . father": Oates, p. 17

38 "he pursued . . . amazed": Donald, p. 41

"The more natural . . . nature": Bingham, p. 10

"winked out": Donald, p. 50

"Lincoln had . . . friends": Donald, p. 42

39 "went at it": Donald, p. 51

40 "went at it in good earnest": Donald, p. 53

"He read . . . himself": Donald, p. 55

41 "the right . . . Constitution": Donald, p. 63

"that the institution . . . policy": Donald, p. 64

"of abolitionist . . . evils": Donald, p. 64

5: A House Divided

43 "the most congenial mind": Oates, p. 55

43–44 "Nothing new . . . wonder": Thomas, p. 89

44 "the first . . . better": Sandburg, p. 112
   "He can sit . . . ever met": Sandburg, p. 112
   "pitiless . . . truth": Thomas, p. 99

46 "naturally antislavery . . . feel": Donald, p. 24, 134

47 "had rather . . . South": Stauffer, p. 172
   "sacred": Donald, p. 63
   "a great moral . . . master": McPherson, p. 56

49 "natural death": Donald, p. 134
   "The Kansas-Nebraska Act . . . stunned": Donald, p. 168
   "had never . . . before": Oates, p. 108
   "the monstrous . . . another": Donald, p. 176
   "If all . . . institution": Donald, p. 167

50 "obvious violence . . . recognize it": Donald, p. 201
   "to say all . . . happiness": Donald, p. 202
   "We think . . . overrule this": Donald, p. 201

52 "course of ultimate extinction": Donald, p. 206
   "A house . . . as well as South": Donald, p. 206
   "Well and wisely . . . land": Oakes, p. 5

52–53 "Liberty and slavery . . . Hell": Oakes, p. 37

6: Debating the Future of Slavery in America

55 "I do not . . . equal": Oates, p. 153
   "This government . . . white men": Donald, p. 210
   "Let us . . . equal": Oakes, p. 129

56 "vast moral evil": Oates, p. 150
   "the high road to extinction": Oates, p. 150
   "black Republican": Oates, p. 153

56–57 "I found . . . principles": Oakes, p. xv

58 "I am not . . . people": Donald, p. 221

58 "the difference . . . think it wrong": Donald, p. 223
   "That is . . . world": Donald, p. 224
   "The fight . . . defeats": Donald, p. 229

59 "was going . . . alive": Life & Times, p. 319
   "murder . . . Virginia": Life & Times, p. 309

60 "All over . . . marching on": Life & Times, p. 324

61 "a man . . . doctrine": Stauffer, p. 162

62 "ten thousand . . . any other": Stauffer, p. 162
   "Abolitionist . . . against it": McFeely, p. 208
   "I cannot support Lincoln": Oakes, p. 89

7: Emancipation

65 "hold, occupy, and possess": Oates, p. 221

66 "I never . . . flags": McPherson, p. 274
   "There are . . . traitors": McPherson, p. 274
   "God be praised . . . liberty": Stauffer, pp. 221–22
   "Every slave . . . behind them": "Across the Great Divide," Time, June 26, 2005

67 "We didn't . . . flag back": Stauffer, p. 256

68 "Free every slave . . . institutions": McPherson, p. 358

69 "We have . . . separated": Stauffer, p. 17
   "pride of race . . . hypocrisy": Oakes, p. 194
   "distinct races . . . humanity": Stauffer, p. 17

70 "I can only . . . to go": Oakes, pp. 299–300
   "You need . . . the slaves": Oakes, p. 307

70–71 "fit and necessary war measure": Stauffer, p. 157

72 "It would do . . . would follow": Oakes, p. 168
   "act of justice . . . necessity": Donald, p. 407
   "are and henceforward . . . free": Stauffer, p. 243
   "We shout . . . decree": Stauffer, p. 243

72–73 "Slavery . . . Forever Free": Oakes, p. 197

74 "I claim . . . controlled me": Donald, p. 9
  "I never . . . this paper": Stauffer, p 269

75 "We won't . . . everybody else": Stauffer, p. 266

8: "Mr. Douglass . . . I Am Glad to See You"

77 "would turn . . . for us": Oakes, p. 204

78 "Young men . . . army": Oakes, p. 206

79 "The bravery . . . troops": Oakes, p. 207

80 "made Fort Wagner . . . Yankees": McPherson, p. 686
  "By arming . . . Confederacy": McPherson, p. 687
  "to go . . . Lincoln": *Life & Times*, p. 346

81 "manner . . . earnest": McFeely, p. 228
  "Regulations . . . officers": Stauffer, p. 10

82 "a cause . . . place": McFeely, p. 228
  "difficulties . . . surmounted": Stauffer, p. 10

82–85 "The stairway was crowded . . . without reserve or doubt": Douglass described his first meeting with Lincoln in a letter to abolitionist George L. Stearns, written on August 12, 1863, two days after the meeting; in a speech, "Our Work Is Not Done," delivered before the American Anti-Slavery Society in Philadelphia, December 3–4, 1863 (available online); and in greater detail in his third autobiography, *Life & Times*, first published in 1881, eighteen years after he met the president. Lincoln's secretary, John Hay, referred to the meeting in his diary, while Lincoln left no account. My narrative is based on "Our Work Is Not Done," pp. 6–8; *Life & Times*, pp. 347–49; Stauffer, pp. 19–22; Oakes, pp. 213–15; McFeely, pp. 347–49.

85 "one of . . . America": Stauffer, p. 284
  "Mr. Douglass . . . me": Stauffer, p. 24

9: Lincoln's Secret Plan

87 "We are . . . times": Sandburg, p. 539
  "When This Cruel War Is Over": Stauffer, p. 276

88 "Our bleeding . . . insurgents": McPherson, p. 762
  "I am going . . . beaten": McPherson, p. 771
  "The tide . . . against us": McPherson, p. 769
  "two special . . . slavery": Sandburg, p. 543

88–89 "If they . . . come what will": McPherson, p. 769

89 "the emancipation . . . rebellion": Stauffer, p. 280
  "I need . . . most gladly": *Life & Times*, p. 358

90 "in an alarmed condition": Stauffer, p. 286

90–91 "The slaves . . . hour after this": *Life & Times*, pp. 358–59

91–92 "treated me . . . remarkable man": Stauffer, p. 290

92 "a deeper . . . by him": *Life & Times*, p. 358
  "Every slave . . . loyal cause": Stauffer, p. 290

93 "All hesitation . . . Lincoln": Oakes, p. 234
  "a King's cure . . . evils": Oakes, p. 404

95 "wept like children": McPherson, p. 840
  "*Sound . . . are free*": Oakes, p. 405

10: "My Friend Douglass"

97 "cheer upon cheer . . . the scene": Donald, p. 565

98 "cause of the war . . . all nations": The full text of Lincoln's second inaugural address can be found online at www.bartleby.com/124/pres32.html and at other websites.
  "wonderfully quiet, earnest, and solemn": *Life & Times*, p. 363

98–100 "Though no colored . . . glad you liked it!": *Life & Times*, pp. 365–66

100 "Guns are firing . . . fairly captured it": Donald, p. 581

100–101 "A dreadful disaster . . . kindly voice":
Oakes, p. 243

101 "to leave . . . born": Oakes, p. 269

102 "His greatest . . . countrymen": Oakes, p. 271

103 "He was . . . climbed": Oakes, p. 258

Appendix: "Dialogue Between a Master and Slave"

104 This facsimile of the original document
appears in Caleb Bingham, *The Columbian
Orator,* and is in the public domain.

Picture Credits

The following unique photographs also appear in my book *Lincoln: A Photobiography*: 37, 42 (both), 100. They come from the Library of Congress and are in the public domain, as is 41, which appears in *Lincoln: A Picture Story of His Life* by Stefan Lorant, 1969.

Art Resource, NY: 57, 101

Bildarchiv Preussischer Kulturbesitz/Art Resource, NY: 38

Bridgeman-Giraudon/Art Resource, NY: 39

The Columbian Orator (1816), 10

Library Company of Philadelphia, 78

Library of Congress: viii, 8, 14, 16, 18, 30–31, 36, 37, 40, 42 (both), 45, 48, 51, 54, 58, 60, 61, 63, 67, 71, 74, 76, 82, 84, 86, 91, 95, 96, 99, 100

Life and Times of Frederick Douglass, 1881: 23, 28

Madison County Historical Society, Oneida, NY: 27

Moorland-Spingarn Research Center, Howard University: 79 (both)

National Park Service, Frederick Douglass National Historic Site: 102

National Portrait Gallery, Smithsonian Institution/Art Resource, NY: ii (right), 26

New Bedford Whaling Museum: 24

The New York Public Library/Art Resource, NY: ii (left)

Photographs and Prints Division, Schomburg Center for Research in Black Culture, The New York Public Library, Astor, Lenox and Tilden Foundation: 4, 81

Picture Collection, The New York Public Library, Astor, Lenox and Tilden Foundation: 6, 46, 59, 64, 73, 93, 94

Réunion des Musées Nationaux/Art Resource, NY: 75

SEF/Art Resource, NY: 32

Stock Sales, WGBH/Scala/Art Resource, NY: 53

U.S. Army Military History Institute: 68, 69

Index

Page numbers in *italics* refer to photos and illustrations.

DATE DUE

PRINTED IN U.S.A.